Changing the Curriculum

CURRICULUM STUDIES

General Editor: David Jenkins

Changing
the Curriculum

Barry MacDonald and Rob Walker

Open Books
London

First published in 1976 by Open Books Publishing Limited, 87-89
Shaftesbury Avenue, LONDON WIV 7AD

© Barry MacDonald and Rob Walker 1976
Hardback: ISBN   0 7291 0055 3
Paperback: ISBN   0 7291 0050 2

0032479

98236

374
MAC

Filmset in Linotron 11 pt Baskerville by
G. A. Pindar & Son Ltd, Scarborough, N. Yorkshire
Printed in Great Britain by The Pitman Press, Bath

Contents

Editor's introduction

Curriculum studies is one of the growth points in education today. In essence it takes as problematic what should be planned, taught and learned in our schools. It is a central and centralising study organised around the choices facing the practitioner. It can be gritty and ragged about the edges, lacking the settled conceptual apparatus of other disciplines in education, but it aspires to being *usable*. Curriculum studies is a recognition of the needs felt by practitioners for better ways of describing, explaining and justifying what goes on in educational programmes. The question *What ought we to be teaching in our schools?* is a more complex one than appears at first glance: this series explores the underlying complexities.

There are perhaps two major reasons for the present upsurge of interest in curriculum theory and practice. The first is that we have just completed in British education the first cycle of the curriculum reform movement (a cycle brought to an end by the current financial stringency); this movement brought to the surface a number of pressing issues – it was never simply a question of updating the knowledge component. There have been two main trends in the analysis of the 'curriculum reform' phenomenon. The first stresses the movement as an attempt to *institutionalise* the whole process of curriculum change and seeks to explore the full implications of making the curriculum into a legitimate object of social policy. The second points to the 'grass roots' image of reform and characterises the curriculum reform movement in terms of the emergence of 'curriculum entrepreneurs', first-generation project directors who backed hunches derived from their own experience. Both accounts raise problems. The first suggests that the principal issue is a boundary dispute over professional autonomy between administrators and teachers. The second invites us to view the curriculum reform movement as a free enterprise system in which change agents invent and disseminate classroom novelty in the teeth of an inadequate infrastructure for planned change. But neither of these 'social movement' perspectives is much help in generating the kind of research tradition that would allow us to explore the conflicting premises behind alternative proposals.

The second reason for the upsurge in interest to some extent complements the first. I refer to the emergence of a 'community of discourse' in the universities, in the schools, in the colleges of education and the teachers' centres, which have become seriously interested in curriculum as an area of study. This is not to suggest that the 'practical' reform movement spawned a derivative 'theoretical' literature, for the same people were frequently involved in both. Indeed such an overlap is wholly appropriate given the aspiration of curriculum studies to be a theory about practice – and a practitioners' theory. One sign of the emerging 'community of discourse' has been the proliferation of courses in curriculum, both in-service and as part of initial training.

This series is an attempt to explore the main issues likely to recur in curriculum studies courses. Its authors have all been involved directly in curriculum reform, either as teachers, project members or evaluators. All are familiar with the world of the classroom. Most have many years of teaching experience (in my own case over eight in a South Wales comprehensive school) and all are currently involved in preparing and teaching curriculum studies in teacher education.

Although part of a series, each book is capable of standing on its own. All have end-of-chapter summaries, and suggestions for further reading.

This particular volume, *Changing the Curriculum,* was written by Barry MacDonald and Rob Walker. Barry MacDonald went to the Centre for Applied Research in Education at the University of East Anglia as evaluator on the Nuffield/Schools Council Humanities Curriculum Project. He is at present director of a number of project evaluations, notably UNCAL (an acronym for Understanding Computer Assisted Learning), the independent evaluation of the National Development Programme in Computer Assisted Learning, and SAFARI (an acronym for Success and Failure and Recent Innovation). Rob Walker, his colleague on SAFARI, was previously at the Centre for Science Education at Chelsea College, University of London, and is particularly interested in classroom research. MacDonald and Walker have pioneered a new approach to the ethics of the case study, which requires that close-up portrayals of innovations in action should first be negotiated and cleared with the research subjects themselves, and prefers the role of the honest broker to that of the judge.

Changing the Curriculum summarises the issues to be faced at the end of the first phase of the curriculum reform movement. Although the authors hold back from making major recommendations arising from their research, it is clear that a gap exists between the rhetoric of curriculum renewal and its realities, a gap traced through the vicissitudes of several projects involved in the innovation game.

David Jenkins

Acknowledgements

Since 1973 we have both been working on the Ford Foundation SAFARI Project (the acronym stands for 'Success and Failure and Recent Innovation'), located at the Centre for Applied Research in Education at the University of East Anglia.

The SAFARI Project has attempted, through detailed case studies of curriculum developments in action, to identify the effects of curriculum reform on the education system – at a national level, in L.E.A.s, schools and classrooms. Our work in SAFARI informs this book in its content and in its analyses, and we would like to take this opportunity to acknowledge our debts:

To the directors and team members of the Geography for the Young School Leaver Project; the Nuffield Science Teaching Project (and in particular Nuffield Secondary Science); the Humanities Curriculum Project; and Project Technology, without whose active help and assistance and the cooperation of many people associated with the projects nationally, regionally and locally, little of our research would have been possible.

To the Ford Foundation.

To our colleagues on SAFARI: John Elliott, Helen Simons, Lawrence Stenhouse, Robert Stake and Hans Brügelman.

To the Schools Council and the Nuffield Foundation.

To the many individuals and organisations who have helped and encouraged us in our work. Only a few are mentioned in the book but very many more have contributed to our ideas and influenced our thinking.

To Sheila and Lynne, Tracey, Shelley, Ben and Thomas.

In addition the authors and publishers would like to thank:

Ronald G. Havelock for permission to quote from *Planning for Innovation through Dissemination and the Utilization of Knowledge* (Ann Arbor, Center for Research on the Utilizations of Scientific

Knowledge, University of Michigan). Trevor Higginbottom for permission to quote from a paper, 'Managing the Change', delivered to a CRITE (Council for Research in Teacher Education) conference in September 1975.

The National Centre for School Technology for permission to use a diagram from 'School Technology Forum No 1'.

David Jenkins, general editor, for helpful comments and constructive pressure to meet deadlines.

Kirsten May for secretarial support.

INTRODUCTION

In the summer of 1961 a private British charity called the Nuffield Foundation was persuaded to donate some money to a group of teachers who wanted to 'do something' about the grammar school science curriculum. The teachers belonged to the Science Masters' Association, one of whose leading members had just come back from a visit to Russia and America – where he had been astonished to find school courses in nuclear physics. The Nuffield Foundation's involvement in the development of new school curricula was soon to become a landmark in the education system. Suddenly, in England and Wales, much of the planning and energy that since the second world war had been devoted to implementing the Education Act of 1944 was switched to the problem of curriculum obsolescence. Whitehead's dictum 'The rule is absolute – the nation that does not value trained intelligence is doomed' assumed the status of an imperative, and a decade of planned educational change began.

The Nuffield initiative set the wheels of the state turning, and in 1964 a new institution appeared, one that has since become a familiar if still contentious feature in the formal structure of the school system. This was the Schools Council for Curriculum and Examinations. In the space of twelve years the Schools Council has initiated and supported more than 160 projects whose major concern has been to lend speed and quality to the ongoing process of curriculum change in the classroom by centralising the functions of invention and production. The implicit model of planned change was thus centre-peripheral: innovation is accelerated at the centre, then disseminated to the outposts.

Fifteen years after Nuffield took the first step, we can now look back and try to develop a perspective upon this effort; to draw back a little from it until we achieve focus. The time is propitious: the curriculum development movement is, at present, in 'cold storage', awaiting an economic thaw. The treasury 'wombles' are out in force, sniffing for the spoor of educational waste and driving innovative spirits into hibernation. Changes of educational practice continue, as they always have done, but systematic and organised curriculum innovation on the centre-periphery model appears to have lost much of its early momentum. The severe economic recession we have now entered entails not only a reduction of the material resources required at all levels to support such systems, but also an erosion of their psychological foundations. The buoyancy and the optimism that an expanding economy generates within a culture have gone.

This book is an attempt to describe and understand the process of planned curriculum change that we have experienced over the past fifteen years. The process has reached a hiatus, perhaps a permanent halt, and it may be that the day of the national curriculum development project is over. On the other hand, centralised curriculum innovation preceded a current feature of educational systems throughout the western hemisphere – the increasing degree of intervention by government agencies in the affairs of teachers. It is perhaps too soon to close the story, too premature to assume that the 'centre-periphery' model is dead.

We have tried in the chapters that follow to chart the history of the curriculum development movement, to explicate its theories, and to describe its processes and structures in action. The last decade has seen a change of mood. The optimism of the pioneer innovators is now muted, in part because planned change has turned out to be a more formidable problem than was initially assumed.

We start from a view of curriculum development as the systematic planning, production and use of new practice; and see attempts to institutionalise new practice as a central feature of the change process. Our focus is on curriculum change as an example of the more general phenomenon of planned social change. We approach the curriculum reform movement from two different perspectives. First we look at theories which have been developed to account for the processes of social invention, transmission and implementation; not just in curriculum

2

development but more generally in the area of planned social change. We also consider those aspects of the social history of the post-war period, both here and in the U.S.A., which provide a context for understanding the relevance of the theories to contemporary events. Second, we attempt to describe the process of curriculum change by looking at three case studies. In these case studies we are able to portray the people and events that constitute the process of change in a fine-grained descriptive detail that complements the global view provided by theory.

The curriculum reform movement is one lens through which it is possible to view the processes of change in education. It is not the only lens. Indeed it is possible to argue that the drama of the project is dependent on the groundswell of less ostentatious developments within many classrooms, and that in the past we have overestimated the contribution of the project to the climate of change. The case studies allow the reader to some extent to judge for himself.

The story is a complex one. The world of curriculum reform perhaps once seemed more straightforward. But there has been a radical transformation of assumptions and expectations even during the brief lifetime of the Schools Council. Two quotations may illustrate this transformation. The first is imputed to Derek Morell, the first joint secretary of the Council, and a primary source of much of its initial institutional adrenalin: 'Never mind the plan, let's get the ideas right; everything else will follow.' The second comes from Jack Wrigley, former director of the Council's Research Section. In a letter to the *Times Educational Supplement* on 25 September 1975 Wrigley wrote 'It is fairly easy to have a bright idea – less easy in the sphere of the Schools Council to see that idea to fruition.'

The chapters that follow explore the space in time and in understanding between these words. We begin, however, not with the projects themselves but at a more general level with theories of innovation and social change. This review sets the scene for considering the curriculum reform movement as a social movement. The bulk of this volume goes on to analyse three major British curriculum projects in an attempt to discover an adequate basis for tentative generalisations. We conclude with appraisal of the social context for curriculum innovation in the mid-1970s, and speculate briefly about the future.

1 THE DIFFUSION OF INNOVATION — MODELS AND THEORIES

Why start with theory, rather than action? Why the diffusion of innovation, rather than its invention? Fair questions. Let us venture answers. In some fields of education, theory is fully developed, sophisticated, complex and demanding. Such theory can trap the beginner, offering him elegant substitutes for his own analyses of and reflections upon the phenomena they address. Or it may undermine the student who seeks his own understanding of the field, interposing a set of baffling obstacles between him and the data. The somewhat daunting title of this opening chapter may suggest that we have such a hurdle in store. Not so. Innovation theory will strike the reader, as it strikes us, as crude and simplistic, notable for its reach rather than its grasp. This is not to denigrate the efforts of the theorists. They have made a start, and for that we should be thankful. They have thrown up a range of ideas, parameters and insights which we can use, as they do, in the attempt to comprehend an important part of our experience, of what we do and what is done to us. But, and it is a significant 'but', their maps are primitive. To read them is to appreciate how little distance we have travelled on the road to understanding and explanation; how far there is to go. The reader, we feel, will not be daunted by entering the field of innovation through its theory; on the contrary, we are sure that the framework it offers will prove not only useful, but a stimulus to independent thought.

Why the diffusion of innovation? Because the question of how new ideas and practices spread from their point of origin and gain widespread adoption is central to any system of planned change on a large scale. The enduring problem that has plagued the sponsors and planners of curriculum innovation is not the

4

problem of creation, but the problem of impact, the failure to achieve anything like the mass conversion to new aims, new content, and new approaches that they aspire to. The schools have not, it seems, been transformed by all the organised, systematised, specialised efforts of the professional innovators. Could it be that more understanding is needed of how *un*planned educational change comes about? This possibility is drawing more and more of those concerned with curriculum innovation to consider studies of the change process, not only in education but in other fields, and in society as a whole.

Such studies are in plentiful supply, as we shall see, but relatively few concern educational change, and almost all of these have been carried out in countries other than Britain. What is more, their theoretical yield is generally meagre, so much so that we have to resort largely to second-order theorists, those who have drawn theory from summarisations of large numbers of limited studies conducted by other people. The Americans Rogers and Shoemaker (1971) and Ronald Havelock (1971), whose work is featured in this chapter, come into this category. Although the breadth of their data bases may constitute in some respects a strength, it is also arguably a weakness. Donald Schon (1971) and Ernest House (1974) are the two other theorists we have chosen to feature, Schon because his Reith Lectures about the 'centre-periphery' model of diffusion have been widely quoted in discussions of innovation, and House because his theories are based upon extensive experience of the American curriculum innovation system. We hope that the British reader will not be deterred by the fact that all of our featured theorists are American. In the next chapter, where we undertake a brief history of the curriculum development movement, we are concerned with the parallel movement that took place in the U.S.A. An understanding of that experience should help us to use the theory with discrimination and profit.

That the curriculum reform movement presented opportunities for the study of social change was not lost on American observers. The point was made explicitly by Miles in his introduction to *Innovation in Education* (1964):

The relatively high rate of educational innovation we are now experiencing provides an excellent opportunity to understand the problems of innovation in educational systems with some clarity. It seems fair to say that, while a substantial body of empirical information on change in social systems of various sizes has accumulated, there is no really adequate theory of social change. Thus the current situation presents a fertile ground for enquiry, and there is a very real possibility that our theoretical understanding of social change can be overhauled and refined.

Indeed the 'opportunity' was, even as Miles wrote, being exploited, notably by Richard Carlson (1965) in his study of the diffusion of modern mathematics.

Inkeles (1964), writing at about the same time in his *What is Sociology?*, depicts a general shift away from all-embracing theories of change, such as Marxist explanations, towards more limited-scope studies, dealing with change more concretely 'as it manifests itself in different types of social organisation under various conditions'.

This decline in the search for (new) global theories, as Inkeles suggests, has been accompanied by a near-explosive proliferation of empirical studies of particular change processes, most of them concerned with aspects of industrialisation, and many of them assimilable within the definition of social change suggested by Rogers and Shoemaker (1971) in their exhaustive survey of diffusion research, *Communication of Innovation*. This is an important definition and worth stressing, since much of the subsequent argument of this chapter hinges on examining its assumptions and considering various extensions of – and alternatives to – the Rogers and Shoemaker position.

The process of social change consists of three sequential steps: (1) invention, (2) diffusion, (3) consequences. Invention is the process by which new ideas are created or developed. Diffusion is the process by which these new ideas are communicated to the members of a social system. Consequences are the changes that occur within a social system as a result of the adoption or rejection of the innovation. Change occurs when a new idea's use or rejection has an effect. Social change is therefore an effect of communication.

Subsequent criticisms of the model were on the grounds of its inadequacy (acknowledged by the authors themselves) as an

6

account of innovation process in which additional stages of development, integration or reinterpretation feature prominently. But Rogers and Shoemaker recognised that they were operating within a deficient research tradition, and on the basis of their survey put in a plea for a 'theory' of planned change able to account for the fact that it takes place typically within bureaucratic structures. They write:

> One of the distinctive aspects of educational diffusion is that it often occurs in bureaucratic structures. Many more of the innovation-decisions are authority or collective decisions rather than optional innovation-decisions, but most of the past research has treated educational innovations as if they were individually adopted, even though many are not. A further shortcoming of the education tradition is that researchers have largely ignored (1) consideration of communication channels, and (2) how the social structure acts to impede not facilitate diffusion. These conceptual shortcomings need to be overcome in future studies of educational diffusion.

Nor does the Rogers and Shoemaker model deal with the process of decay very well. But then an invention like the combine harvester is not readily susceptible to reinterpretation, nor does it, over time and distance, degenerate into a hand-sickle, and their survey is not primarily, or even substantially, concerned with educational innovations, in which such processes are often of central concern. This is not to suggest that for students of educational innovation more general examinations of diffusion are profitless.

We now want to examine in more detail the contribution made by three theorists in the field of curriculum change, Havelock, Schon and House. All developed models for the processes of invention, diffusion or dissemination, models which, as we have said, are to varying extents helpful or inadequate, misleading or stimulating. But in a new field these models and these theories are all we've got. The argument of this book is that we need to be attentive to curriculum change and social change as and when it occurs. But we begin with some of the existing frameworks of explanation that have been generated.

Ronald Havelock: three models of change

Havelock's book *Planning for Innovation through the Dissemination and Utilisation of Knowledge* (1971) begins by acknowledging his debt to Rogers's *The Diffusion of Innovations* (1962), but then draws attention to some important distinctions. Although Rogers was aware that his ideas have practical applicability, his primary audience was the academic research community. Havelock, in contrast, aimed his writing explicitly at the practitioners and policymakers. There were other differences: Rogers restricted his survey to empirical research findings, while Havelock includes anecdotes, untested theories and some case studies. Also, Rogers limits himself largely to considering the diffusion of products or specific practices. It could be argued that in doing so he took too narrow a view, for this way of construing innovation has the disadvantage that it neglects social/psychological research in influence systems, attitude formation, and human behaviour in groups or organisations.

The major conclusion from Havelock's review of four thousand studies is that they can be grouped according to how their authors view the dissemination and utilisation process. Havelock offers a three model classification, comprising a 'Social Interaction' perspective, a 'Research, Development and Diffusion' perspective, and a 'Problem-solving' perspective. So much discussion of the problems and strategies of curriculum reform has referred to Havelock's models that it is worth having a close look at them. Figure 1.1 is reproduced from Havelock, who has this to say about each model:

Social Interaction (S-I)

An innovation . . . is presented or brought to the attention of a potential receiver population. The receiver and the receiver's needs are defined and determined exclusively by the sender. The receiver is supposed to react to the new information, and the nature of his reaction determines whether or not subsequent stages will occur. If his awareness is followed by an expression of interest, he is launched on a series of stages which terminate with acceptance or rejection of the innovation. The diffusion of the innovation depends greatly upon the channels of communication within the receiver group, since information about the innovation is transmitted primarily through the social interaction of the group members . . .

8

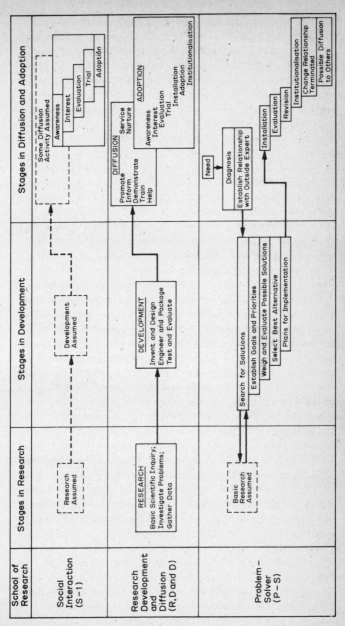

1.1 *Stages Typically Included in Models of Change Within Three Schools of Research.*

9

Authors who consider the process of adoption from this point of view are concerned with the stages through which individuals pass as they reach a decision to adopt an innovation. They are concerned in addition with the related issue of the mechanisms by which the innovation diffuses through the adopting group. Studies in this area have shown that the most effective means of spreading information about an innovation is through personal contact. Thus, the key to adoption is viewed by authors of this school to be the *social interaction* among members of the adopting group.

Research Development and Diffusion (R, D and D)

The Research, Development and Diffusion (R, D and D) perspective looks at the process of change from the point of view of the *originator* of an innovation, and it begins with the formulation of a problem on the basis of a presumed receiver need. The initiative in making this identification, however, is taken by the *developer*, not the receiver, and in this way the R, D and D school is similar to the S-I school. It differs from the S-I school, however, in that it views the process of change from an earlier point in time. The focus is on the activity phases of the developer as he designs and develops a potential solution.

Models which are included in the R, D and D school depict the process of change as an orderly sequence which begins with the identification of a problem, proceeds through activities which are directed towards finding or producing a solution to this problem, and ends with diffusion of this solution to a target group. The initiative in these activities is taken by the researchers, the developers, and the disseminators; the receiver remains essentially passive.

The major emphasis of all theorists in the R, D and D school is on the planning of change on a large scale. This involves detailed development, based on scientific knowledge, and rigorous testing and evaluation . . . It also involves mechanisms for distributing the innovation and installing it in target systems.

Problem-solving (P-S)

In the Problem-Solver perspective the receiver (an individual or a group) initiates the process of change by identifying an area of concern or by sensing a need for change. Once the problem area is identified, the receiver undertakes to alter the situation either through his own efforts, or by recruiting suitable outside assistance. Whereas the receiver in the S-I and R, D and D models is passive, the receiver in the P-S model is actively involved in finding an innovation to solve his own problem. Specifically what the new input will be is determined largely by the receiver himself; whether or not this same input could also satisfy the needs of other receivers (i.e. mass diffusion) is not generally considered.

. . . this school is primarily concerned with those cases in which the assistance of outside resources is utilised; these resources are likely to be individuals or groups which can generally be referred to as 'change agents'.

The relationship between sender and receiver is one of collaboration, and whereas in the S-I and the R, D and D models the receiver was referred to as the 'target system', it is here called the 'client system'. The client system may range in size from an individual person to an entire nation.

It can be seen at once that a critical dimension of variance among the three models is the degree of compliance ascribed to the so-called 'receiver', and, by association, the degree of control over the change process exerted by outsiders seeking to introduce new ideas. Tony Becher (1971) of the Nuffield Foundation, the pioneer sponsors of the curriculum development movement in this country, defined the role of central innovative agencies within each of Havelock's models in this way: 'In the research, development and diffusion model the external change agent is concerned mainly with preparing and disseminating packaged solutions. In the social interaction model he concentrates on identifying and strengthening communication networks and promoting the exchange of ideas. And in the problem-solving model he acts as a resource consultant, working in a non-directive relationship with his clients.'

Becher went on to suggest that to a considerable extent the curriculum movement in Britain had set out with the first of these, evolved into a mixed model incorporating elements of the second, and would in the seventies be characterised by the client-service perspective of the problem-solving model. We shall revisit his views in the next section. Stenhouse (1975) concurs with Becher in favouring the problem-solving model, but

11

wants to encourage a research and development capacity in the clientele. The role of the external agent is to help the client to develop research procedures which will themselves constitute the dissemination package, thus offering a solution or part-solution to the problem of generalisation which Havelock associates with this model. (Those who would discount the Stenhouse prescription as unrealistically ambitious should first take a look at the achievements of John Elliott and Clem Adelman in the Ford Teaching Project (see Ford Teaching Project 1973-5).)

Havelock himself, having identified his three models, ends by articulating a synthesis of the three based on the concept of 'linkage', which stresses user needs and a reciprocal relationship between the user and the resource system. Havelock spells out the implications for policy makers at the national level:

> It is possible to identify and differentiate within our total society a variety of knowledge-building, knowledge-disseminating and knowledge-consuming sub-systems, each with its own distinctive protective skin of values, beliefs, special language and normative behaviours . . . the government should be in a position to see the various sub-cultures as *one system* . . . Government must have the capacity to monitor this macrosystem, facilitating linkage where barriers exist . . . should see to it that all the functions of research, development and diffusion are adequately performed; it should help in the establishment and maintenance of networks of social influence which can move tested innovations towards mass consumption; and it should facilitate effective problem-solving by user and user systems.

This is rather like advising the punter to back every horse in the race to make sure his money is on the winner. Besides, Havelock appears to assume a consensual process of melioration under benevolent overarching management. House, for one, views educational affairs with a somewhat more jaundiced gaze, as we shall see, but first we turn to an analysis of planned change that made a considerable impact on British thinking in 1970: Donald Schon's Reith Lectures. Although it was neither derived from or directed to education, Schon's influence on contemporary theory of curriculum change has been pervasive.

Donald Schon: three models for diffusion

Schon has taken models for diffusion beyond the assumptions embedded in previous models. In *Beyond the Stable State: Public and Private Learning in a Changing Society* (1971) Schon considers the survival requirements of social systems entering a phase of permanent change, and articulates a code of public learning appropriate to such systems. In the course of his analysis he examines models for the diffusion of innovations, taking, rather like Rogers and Shoemaker, a view of social change which has the outward spread of inventions as its key explanatory idea. Schon himself puts the main point neatly: 'Diffusion of innovation is a dominant model for the transformation of societies according to which novelty moves out from one or more points to permeate the society as a whole.'

(1) *The centre-periphery model*

The first of Schon's models, which he calls the 'centre-periphery' model, rests on three basic assumptions:

  (1) The innovation exists, fully realised in its essentials, prior to its diffusion.
  (2) Diffusion is the movement of an innovation from a centre out to its ultimate users.
  (3) Directed diffusion is a centrally managed process of dissemination, training, and the provision of resources and incentives.

In view of the readiness with which first generation Schools Council Curriculum Projects get cited as examples of Schon's centre-periphery model, it is worth noting that Schon's paradigmatic example is the U.S. Agricultural Extension Programme, which successfully increased agricultural productivity in the late nineteenth and early twentieth century. In view of the criticisms that have been directed at agricultural metaphors in curriculum development, and at agricultural models for the spread of innovation, it may be useful to remind ourselves again that as a piece of machinery a novel curriculum is in many respects quite unlike a combine harvester.

The effectiveness of a centre-periphery system, argues Schon, depends among other things on the level of resources at the centre, the number of points at the periphery, the length of the spokes through which diffusion takes place, and the energy required to gain a new adoption. We may feel that 'spoke length' is a rather feeble and unenlightening metaphor, and Schon does not repeat it, talking instead of 'infrastructure technology', and maintaining that the scope of a centre-periphery system varies directly with the level of technology governing the flow of men, materials, money and information. The scope also depends upon the system's 'capacity for generating and managing feedback'. Because the process of diffusion is regulated by the centre, its effectiveness depends upon the ways in which information flows back to the centre.

Simple systems of this kind are prone to failure, says Schon, through resource exhaustion, overload, and mismanagement. 'When the centre-periphery system exceeds the resources or the energy at the centre, overloads the capacity of the radii, or mishandles feedback from the periphery, it fails. Failure takes the form of simple ineffectiveness in diffusion, distortion of the message, or disintegration of the system as a whole.' He instances the pharmaceutical drug salesman who has too many doctors in his quota, and who either spreads his efforts too thinly to gain sales or has insufficient contact with head office and garbles the message. Sales drop, the salesman loses morale, the system falls apart.

(2) *The proliferation of centres model*

Schon goes on to depict his second model of the diffusion process, and calls it the 'proliferation of centres' model. Stenhouse (1975) is among those who have argued that this model most closely corresponds with the facts of curriculum development in England and Wales. It is, suggests Schon, designed as though to extend the limits and overcome the sources of failure inherent in the simpler model. 'This system retains the basic centre-periphery structure but differentiates primary and secondary centres. Secondary centres engage in the diffusion of innovations; primary centres support and manage secondary centres. The effect is to multiply many-fold the reach and efficiency of the diffusion system.' In this model the proliferation of secondary centres provides an exponential increase in the leverage of a given central resource, each new centre creating its own periphery and infrastructure. 'The limits to the reach and effectiveness of the new system depend now on the primary centre's ability to generate, support and manage the new centres.'

Although Schon's examples of this model are industrial

14

expansion, the Communist movement and Imperialism, he adds a comment on the functioning of the system which bears a remarkably close resemblance to the dissemination activities of the Schools Council/Nuffield Foundation Humanities Curriculum Project (see Rudduck, in preparation). At the time of the Reith Lectures the H.C.P. was just getting under way. Schon writes: 'The model of the proliferation of centres makes of the primary centre a *trainer of trainers*. The central message includes not only the content of the innovation to be diffused, but a pre-established method for its diffusion. The primary centre now specialises in training, deployment, support, monitoring and management.'

The resemblance is not sustained when Schon goes on to posit a level of control by the primary centre which has no parallel in British curriculum development although some of the 'quality control' procedures introduced in the American movement were inspired by comparable aspirations. Schon describes, in the context of industrial expansion, the dominant pattern in the primary centre's relationship to secondary centres:

The primary centre is a guardian of pre-established doctrine and methodology. It selects territories for expansion, and deploys and organises agents of expansion.
It is not only the source and model of operations to be diffused but the developer of methodologies of diffusion.
It trains and incubates new agents of diffusion.
It supports decentralised outposts through capital, information and know-how.
It monitors and manages decentralised operations, setting criteria for performance monitoring performance, observing and overseeing leadership in the outposts.
It maintains information throughout the network of outposts.

The sources of failure in the 'proliferation of centres' model are similar to those in the main model. The demands on central management, particularly the central doctrine, may not meet the needs of secondary centre leaders looking for support and flexibility to counter local resistance, and such centres may become detached from the primary centre. When that happens, says Schon, 'the diffusion system fragments and becomes unable to maintain itself and expand. It may still transform dispersed societies. But the information no longer consists in diffusion of an established message. It leads, rather, to a variety of regional transformations which bear only a family resemblance to one another.'

Up to this point, in his treatment of social change, Schon has confined himself to a historical analysis of diffusion systems which became particularly dominant in the late nineteenth century and which were all variants of the centre-periphery type. From this point on, having explicated and illustrated the model, he goes on the attack, alleging that the model has become a prescription for contemporary action, and is entirely inappropriate to contemporary society. Much of the blame for this normative use of the model he lays at the feet of theorists like Rogers, with whose work we began this section. Taking Rogers as the arch-advocate of the centre-periphery model, Schon dismisses as simple-minded Rogers's equation of diffusion with 'communication' (an equation Rogers was, at the time of this attack, preparing to reinforce with a change of title for the second edition). Schon's main attack concentrates on Rogers's neglect of the conflict generated by innovations of broad social significance – innovations which threaten the system as a whole:

> Where the introduction of the innovation requires significant disruption of the entire technological-social system and the system of ideas related to it . . . diffusion of an innovation looks less like the dissemination of information than like a sequence of related disruptions of complex systems, resulting in each case in a new configuration. Here the unit of diffusion is not a product or technique but a whole technological system.

The development and diffusion of new industries qualify for this description in Schon's view, and he adds that non-industrial institutions like education represent developing socio-technical systems of like kind. Such systems grow in interaction with other related systems, usually in unpredictable and therefore unplannable ways. 'The process does not consist primarily in centrally managed dissemination of information.. . . Deliberate entrepreneurial intervention usually intermeshes with the emergence of new demands comparable in their force to the 'dynamic conservatism' (a tendency to fight to remain the same) of the established system itself.' Schon sums up his analysis of the problems of innovation in contemporary society by conceptualising society as a 'dynamically conservative plenum' rather like a dartboard, in which innovations can be ranked as peripheral or central according to the degree of system disruption their acceptance would entail. Rogers's model, he says, fits those minor innovations near the periphery of the plenum but for innovations located near the centre, innovations which precipitate system-wide changes, 'the process of diffusion is a battle for broad and complex transformation. And, within such a process, the assumptions underlying the classical diffusion model do not hold.' The appropriate metaphor for directed diffusion, Schon concludes, is battle rather than communications.

The shifting centres model
Centre-periphery structures, says Schon, are inadequate means of change in the conditions of contemporary western culture. But a 'survival-prone' model has emerged during the twentieth century which may provide a useful guide to the understanding of the change process. This is the 'shifting centres' model, which Schon argues is characteristic of contemporary social movements which operate in 'the interstices of established organisations'. Commenting upon that cluster of interrelated movements which includes civil rights, Black Power, community action, disarmament and student revolt, Schon defines its characteristics as a system of innovation diffusion in the following terms:

> *It has no clearly established centre*; centres appear, reach a peak, and disappear to be replaced by new centres within quite short periods of time.
> *There is no stable, centrally established message*; the message shifts and evolves, producing a family of related messages.
> *The system of the movement cannot be described as centre-periphery*; centres rise and fall, messages change. But the movement is a diffusing, learning system, in which both primary and secondary messages evolve rapidly, along with the organisation of diffusion itself.

All this is made possible by the technology of modern communication systems, which enable participants in the movement to have continuous access, via the media, the telephone and rapid transportation, to shifts of meaning and direction, and to maintain connectedness. Because the structure is loose, it is adaptive to these shifts, and flexible enough to regroup around the 'new'. Ad hoc leadership is by those who articulate the latest move, and cannot be maintained for long, because the leaders cannot control or monopolise the information on which counter-bids for leadership will be based. They don't have time to change the social network into an organisation (which might permit such control) before a new transformation occurs.

Stenhouse (1975) does not share Schon's enthusiasm about the potential of the 'movement' as a paradigm for educational policy, arguing that within its structure there is no systematic basis for the critical development of the message. Stenhouse maintains that 'a central problem in the improvement of educa-tion is the gap between accepted policy and practice.' Such a formulation would not, however, seem to deal with Schon's main point of the whole book, that the notion of 'accepted policy' implies a degree of stability which has ceased to be functional in our society. We shall have occasion to refer back to some of these comments of Schon later, when we consider the models of cur-riculum dissemination employed by the Geography for the Young School Leaver Project.

This brief survey of the literature can now be completed with a look at the work of Ernest House. The reader should note that all the leading theorists in this field are American. By devoting as much attention as we have to theories about the spread of innovations we are implicitly advocating more attention to theory. At the same time we should endorse the warning given by Rogers and Shoemaker, and repeated by Schon, that theory tends to lag behind the realities of emerging practice.

Ernest House: diffusion in urban societies
House is the most recent of the theorists we consider (see espe-cially 1975). His focus is firmly on educational innovation, and to a large extent arises out of personal experience of the cur-riculum reform movement. He is able to take into account nearly a decade of attempts to implement one major variant of the centre-periphery model, the R, D and D paradigm first iden-tified by Havelock.

Although he offers no new model of innovation diffusion (locating his perspective firmly within Havelock's social interaction school and utilising concepts formulated mostly by other change analysts), House takes the theory of 'personal contact', which derived largely from studies of innovation in rural societies, and updates it, showing how some characteristic phenomena of urbanisation, such as changes in transportation, population distribution and social group structure, impact on the functioning of the process in the field of educational innovation. 'The rural population is homogeneously spread out so that "contagious" diffusion (one person talking to another person similar in social status) is the rule. In such cases the major factor limiting personal contact and, hence, innovation spread, is distance.' House contrasts this with urban society: 'As urbanisation increases, population density shifts and becomes more heterogeneous; barriers such as social status become more significant than distance in impeding personal communication.' Here, House contends, the pattern of spread changes; instead of regular waves emanating from fixed points, as in rural diffusion, innovations leap from one concentration of population to the next largest in size, independent of distance. House calls this the urban hierarchy of distribution and, although the pattern does not exclude some 'contagious' diffusion, it is size that predominates over distance. Paradoxically the theories of House were derived initially from the work of the Swedish geographer Torsten Hagerstrand (1973) whose spatial models were constructed to explain the spread of agricultural inventions.

What is involved in this change of pattern is a change in the adopting unit. House uses the term 'household' to describe those innovations (typical of rural studies) which are essentially adopted by individuals, and the term 'entrepreneurial' to describe the urban innovation, where the typical adopting unit is an institution, or town, or administrative group. In educational terms, teachers are associated with household innovations, administrators with entrepreneurial ones. The 'entrepreneur' in this sense can be seen as Schon's secondary centre leader, a change agent or advocate of the innovation within the system. Diffusion hinges on the presence and distribution of potential entrepreneurs.
Pursuing the implications of urbanisation for the personal contact theory of diffusion, House says:

The social structure is the dominating force. In organisations, only top-level administrators have numerous external direct contacts. In schools, only a few administrators participate freely in such information flows. Teachers are greatly restricted in their professional contacts, and the effect of such restrictions . . . is to reduce greatly innovation diffusion between towns, organisations, and schools.

The problem for innovation diffusion, House argues, is how to extend the contact networks of teachers and break down the barriers that prevent the formation of personal contact networks that cut across levels of the educational hierarchy. Both horizontal transmission by teachers and vertical transmission by administrators are severely impeded by such barriers. A further barrier, though not a new one, is associated with the decentralisation of educational government. Each school district is a separate governmental unit, and the zealousness which protects this autonomy prevents the development of personal contact channels to innovations emanating from the centre.

House goes on to demonstrate how the rational curriculum change model, which has dominated American management of innovation for the past ten years, the R, D and D model, failed to take account of social interaction theory and tried instead to impose a highly depersonalised technocratic model based on role specialisation, a model which in effect decreased personal contact within and between educational structures, reinforcing and extending existing hierarchies and reducing the teacher to the role of passive, non-contagious receiver of innovation. Not only, House suggests, does this have the effect of restricting the flow of innovation, it also increases the likelihood of the teacher modifying the innovation in practice to conform to the norms of his peer group, with whom he is functionally identified. A more effective approach to educational change, House argues, would take account of the urban hierarchy, promoting rapid adoption in the larger regional centres, providing more incentives for local entrepreneurs and increasing the numbers participating in the change enterprise. Above all, the aim should be to

reduce political, social and organisational barriers to contact with the outside world. It is in the nature of organisations to limit such involvement. Giving teachers access to the outside

20

personal contacts that administrators now have would tremendously increase innovation diffusion in education. General urban development will also assist in the process.

House carries the social-interaction analysis extensively into the invention of innovations and into the treatment of innovations within the school, thus responding to some of the weaknesses of this model noted by Havelock. In concentrating much of his attention on collective adaptation and on the structure of educational organisations, he also meets some of the criticisms of Rogers and Shoemaker which we mentioned earlier. Finally, House's view of the change process goes a long way to substantiate Schon's proposition that a metaphor of battle is an apt one. The title of House's book, *The Politics of Educational Innovation*, reflects the degree of conflict which he sees in the process. Educational change is, for House, a product of the interaction of factional groups competing for resources in attempts to influence and control each other and their own members. In the course of his book he engages in an extensive exploration of the relationship between the American educational and economic systems, an exploration he concludes by stressing what he sees to be the dangers of accepting 'national goals' for education, dangers he associates with attempts to make education serve more directly and narrowly the drive for economic expansion. The contemporary innovation system he defines as basically an attempt by the centre to capture control of the periphery by exerting a 'cultural totalitarianism'. 'Inherent in the process is the production of standardised materials for a mass market, which the logic of large scale economics demands. It is difficult to see how education can be personalised or how the pluralism and diversity of culturally different groups can be respected under such conditions.'

With Schon and House we seem to be much closer to contemporary realities of the social system than with earlier theorists. Schon's concern is with the obsolescence of structures in a period of rapid, uncontrollable and unpredictable change. For him speed of response is the key problem, and fluidity of form the condition of its attainment. House is concerned with diffusion systems as instruments of control which suppress the innovative spirit and the legitimate expression of diversity. He calls, with little optimism, for 'ecological gentleness' and respect for per-

21

sons. Both men view politics and power relationships as key concepts in the analysis of the change process; both argue that new ideas diffuse most effectively on personal networks which are not readily susceptible to systematic organisation and control; but, whereas Schon is confident that attempts to impose and maintain central control of change will fail, House, for all his pungent criticism of the ineffectiveness of centre-periphery control systems, still fears their eventual success, and is not content with the thought that 'the blade of grass will break the concrete.'

Concluding comment

This brief encounter with some of the more notable innovation theorists was intended to provide the reader with a tentative framework to explore through subsequent chapters. The field is wide open in a sense, and we can only hope there is enough substantive data in what follows to support the generation of concepts and models other than those already current, or those we have to offer. We are well aware of the problems that attend theory building, not the least of which is that the fact of social change itself may render the theory of social change obsolete. Our data is by definition out of date: our educational present is not your educational present; people, roles, pathways and institutions will have altered in ways that only you can evaluate and take account of. Book learning is always learning about the past; in our case failure to communicate this, and its implications, would be ironic. We expect our views to be overtaken by events; we hope however that they will help you to identify what those events might be.

Further reading

In this chapter we have attempted to condense a rather diffuse and sometimes inaccessible area of educational literature. For further reading we recommend the major studies cited, particularly Rogers (1962), Rogers and Shoemaker (1971), Schon (1971), House (1974) and Miles (1964), all of which present far more complex pictures than the brief sketches drawn in this review.

2 VARIATIONS ON A THEME – THE EMERGENCE OF CURRICULUM INNOVATION SYSTEMS IN BRITAIN AND AMERICA

Elephants occasionally give birth shortly after rabbits, but few of those who have noted this relationship have been misled into thinking either that the elephant got the idea from the rabbit or that the gestation periods were identical. Nor, if you'll forgive the pun, has the 'issue' been confused. But the closely consecutive emergence of national curriculum innovation systems in America and Britain has given rise to such misconceptions (to heap pun upon pun) and our decision to treat the two together may suggest a sequential view of the two events that we do not in fact hold. On the whole we regard them as an example of parallel innovation, and we believe that our account of the genesis of the Nuffield science reforms substantiates this proposition (see chapter 4).

But there are advantages to be gained from developing an inclusive framework, not least the opportunity to identify how our own cultural idiosyncracies have shaped and differentiated our responses to a commonly perceived problem. It also seems useful to treat the systems chronologically, which will mean beginning with the American system and moving on to the British. In this sense we are dealing with them *as if they were* in lock-step relationship, while holding that they are not. The hope is that this will prove instructive and not simply perverse. Given that we began by devoting some attention to the analyses and concerns of a number of American-based theorists of innovation, we are confident this procedure will at least help to maintain the links between theory and practice.

Diffusion rates in educational systems are slow – slower than in industrial or agricultural systems. New practices, historians have concluded, take about fifty years to spread through one national system (Miles 1964). Some innovations, particularly technological ones like educational television and programmed learning machines, have achieved faster rates, possibly because their attractions are easier to display to prospective clients. But on the whole it's been a leisurely process, far too leisurely to meet the needs of those who, on both sides of the North Atlantic, saw in the fifties and early sixties the need for national intervention in the affairs of the schools to help keep pace with accelerating social change, and to meet shifting national priorities. The mood was one of impatience with natural evolution. Becher (1971) makes the point crisply: 'It has become increasingly evident that we can no longer afford to stumble from one crisis to another, muddling through as best we may: we have to think ahead, to plan carefully, to work out priorities, and to find the most efficient way of meeting these. Change is no longer a matter of random evolution: it has become a question of social engineering.' Or, as one American commentator put it, it was 'Goodbye Mr Chips' (Broudy 1972)

The curriculum movement is popularly dated from the Soviet Union's launching of the first artificial space satellite in October 1957, but it is probably more accurate to define that as a 'triggering' event. The post-war mood of America in the late forties and early fifties, following twenty years of economic depression and war, was one of rising concern about the need for trained manpower in an era of unprecedented scientific development. The progressive movement that had increasingly shaped the American school in the inter-war years came under siege, accused of impoverishing the intellectual climate of schooling and neglecting the education of the gifted, especially the mathematicians, scientists and engineers America would need.

The Massachusetts Institute of Technology was one of the universities that began in the fifties to organise seminars of leading scholars to discuss this problem, following the early lead of the mathematicians who, in 1951, initiated the first federally funded project of the kind that, within a decade, was to be replicated in almost every major discipline. These 'scholarly' initiatives, with their emphasis on academic excellence, found a ready response from middle-class parents. The anticipated post-war economic recession having failed to materialise, there was an expanding and prosperous middle class eager to extend the opportunities and achievements of their college-bound children and ripe for alliance with illustrious scholars from prestigious universities. Critics of the existing system made much of the results of the large-scale testing of recruits that took place in World War II, alleging that these had revealed the near absence of scientific and mathematical comprehension among school graduates (Goodlad 1966).

All that was lacking were the sums of money required to finance the massive task of curriculum revolution. Sputnik 1 was the apocalyptic event that blew open the doors of the federal vault, and precipitated the 'movement'. In 1958 new legislation, in the shape of the National Defense Education Act, not only vastly extended the budget and functions of the Office of Education and its associated agency the National Science Foundation, but also heralded the entry into educational affairs of the Department of Defense, which was to have a significant influence from then on in the management of American social policy. Myron Atkin (1970) has pointed out that the fusion of industrial and military techniques of systems analysis and control that followed the appointment of the president of the Ford Motor Company to the post of Secretary of Defense pervaded the whole of the federal bureaucracy with a belief in social engineering, a faith that, as House (1974) had emphasised, was sustained and made legitimate by the technocratic *élan* of the Kennedy regime.

This was the background and the context which shaped the nature of the 'unholy' alliance that developed between the military/industrial and academic establishments in the 1960s, the alliance that drew up the blueprint for the cold-war curriculum. The temper of the times was crystallised by Harry Broudy (1972) in this anecdote:

> I once jestingly congratulated a noted scholar of Byzantine culture on the irrelevance of his field to the war machine and he informed me indignantly that he had just received a grant to study the effects of certain developments in his field on certain esoteric aspects of the cold war.

The alliance also heralded the development of the dominant paradigm for educational change in the sixties, the so-called R, D and D model referred to earlier. Research, Development and Diffusion was not only a model *of* change; it was also a model *for* change, a blueprint for the future. One of its authors, David Clark (1972), saw it writ large in a scale appropriate to the times: 'The big problem should be faced with a big solution' (quoted in House 1974).

The 'big solution' spawned a multi-million dollar, coast-to-coast system of research and development centres specialising in the generation of new curricula, and regional laboratories whose function was to take these and look after their effective diffusion. The regional laboratories were supposed in theory to attend to local variations of need and circumstances, and to facilitate adaptation as well as adoption. But this system of regional laboratories attracted a cogent critique from House who saw that in practice this function was blocked by those who assigned it:

> As with most government programmes, the central office was never willing to relinquish control. Instead of attending to regional concerns and contexts and perceiving the local peoples as the clients, the labs were forced to attend to central national goals as defined by the Office of Education . . . tight supervision from Washington and uniform annual budgeting procedures kept the labs responding to whatever winds were blowing in Washington and away from the problems of local school personnel. The labs that did not conform lost their funding altogether. More than 50% of the resources of many labs were spent in maintaining liaison with the Office of Education.

Once the curriculum reform movement got into 'third gear' the term 'diffusion', suggesting a natural social process of proliferation, gave way to the term 'dissemination', indicating planned pathways for the transmission of new educational ideas and practices from their point of production to all locations of potential implementation. This change from the notion of diffusion to that of dissemination was not concerned solely with the speed of curriculum evolution, but with its quality too. Matthew Miles, in one of the first major analyses (1964) of educational innovation to follow the post-Sputnik criticisms of the inadequacies of the American public schools, concluded that 'educational innovations are almost never installed on their merits'. He thus confirmed the deepest suspicions of those of his countrymen who sought to wrest control of the American curriculum from the 'Dewey-eyed' educational establishment. To such conservative tastes the problem was not only the need to counter the inertia of the system; it was necessary to reverse the decline brought about by regressive innovation. The planned transmission of expertly produced new programmes seemed a way to introduce some quality control into educational change.

So the concept of dissemination promised both accelerated change and change for the better. In addition, of course, successful dissemination would ensure cost-effectiveness. After all, the high costs of centralised research and development could only be justified by subsequent implementation on a wide scale. This view of dissemination emerged quite clearly in American curriculum developments of the 1960s, which were founded on the principle of finding national answers to questions of national importance in education. The problem was one of disseminating 'right' answers.

'Dissemination' thus implies a simple producer-consumer relationship. There is a curriculum; 'it' is disseminated; 'it' is then used. The 'it' is a stable, fixed entity. If it is not used 'properly' – that is in the way its developers intended it to be used, then 'it' has been adulterated. Although 'adulteration' might well be viewed as 'creativity' by the adulterer, or as intelligent adaptation to individual needs and idiosyncratic circumstances, such innovatory behaviour on the part of the consumer is usually seen by those associated with the production side as regrettable slippage which calls for a strengthening of quality control procedures.

By now the messages coming out of the curriculum reform movement were consistent, pointing to the 'formidable gap between the intent of curriculum projects and what actually happens in classrooms' (see Goodlad 1967). While Goodlad was concerned about the loss of quality in the translation of new curricula into classroom action, a growing number of critics were going further and alleging that no translation was going on. 'Events in the classroom are affected but little by new curriculum packages', despaired Myron Atkin (1970), himself a former curriculum project director. 'It seems that most of the efforts to date have failed or are failing now,' concluded Jack Frymier (1969), a leading member of the educational establishment which had been accused, in the late fifties, of being partly

27

responsible for the alleged decline in academic excellence of the schools. Mario Fantini (1970), an outspoken critic of the elitist rationale of the first decade of the curriculum reform movement, agreed: 'When I visit reality, all I see is continuing failure.'

As such problems, or perceptions, began to mount, the planners' blueprint for curriculum change – a simple three-stage operation consisting of research, development, and diffusion (the so-called R, D and D model) – acquired two further stages: adoption and implementation. Adoption referred to the consumer's 'decision to use' an innovation (usually inferred from his purchase or acquisition of its artefacts) while implementation referred to its realisation. As the difficulties of planned change in social systems began to come home to roost, there was both an evaporation of the heady optimism which had charged the engineers of the first wave of projects, and an extension and reconceptualisation of the task in more hard-headed terms. Consumers were defined as 'targets' and plans of 'attack' were drawn up which typically pivoted round a new functionary known as a 'change agent', who represented the 'intents' of the developers at the local level. It is perhaps hardly surprising that a movement which began with Admiral Rickover (see Cremin 1961) and was liberally endowed by the Department of Defense should eventually assume some of the strategies and the language of the Pentagon.

The American scene provides an interesting backcloth to developments in this country, but also offers a useful comparative perspective helping us to detect which of our assumptions are unique and which shared. It is also worth bearing in mind that a great deal of American thinking and experience has penetrated and influenced events here, perhaps more than is commonly recognised. It will be apparent from our account of Nuffield Science in chapter 4, however, that there is little support for the proposition that the British curriculum reform movement was an imported idea. There was, nevertheless, some movement, both of people and of products, across the Atlantic, a trend that appears to be intensifying.

Before we switch our attention from America it may be worthwhile considering another aspect of dissemination which is more critical over here, given our cultural assumptions, than in the States. This problematic feature arises when one questions the easy assumption that dissemination and implementation are technical problems giving rise to purely technical solutions. In fact, these technical problems have been embedded from the start in a public debate about the control of education, a debate focused on the choice between *centralisation* and *state and local control*.

In America it is the legal responsibility of each state to establish and maintain an educational system, a responsibility which it typically delegates to local communities, creating a tradition of lay control through local school boards. It was precisely this 'democratic' tradition that the sudden massive investment of federal and foundation dollars in centralised curriculum factories was seen to threaten. The rhetoric of the interventionists was powerful and appealing; the low quality of scientific education was failing to meet the defence needs of the nation. A powerful counter-rhetoric emerged to out-sloganise the defenders of centralised initiative: that a decentralised system of control was the country's only protection against tyranny. It was a classic opposition of spectres – the enemy without versus the enemy within.

The debate ensured that each of the R, D and D hurdles would be harder to clear. Research and development could survive on national initiatives, but the innovation might then encounter local difficulties when it came to disseminate its products. Thus the stages of the R, D and D model could not be considered in technical terms. The whole exercise was seriously complicated by politically-based opposition to the centre-periphery assumptions of the exercise. There was also some erosion of the original inspiration. By the mid-sixties the space race with Russia, which justified a curriculum reform movement that was both elitist and dedicated to the pursuit of excellence, was beginning to fizzle out, and the pendulum of public concern was already swinging in recoil towards an egalitarian ethic and an anxiety for improvements in the education of the socially disadvantaged. Some of the problems of curriculum dissemination in the 1970s are to do not just with the dissemination of 'right' answers, but with the dissemination of 'white' answers. During the present decade we can expect to see the incipient politicisation of the curriculum debate in America reach fulfilment. One result which many critics of the federal system hope for is nothing less than the death of the industrial metaphor from its own exhaust fumes.

Reformulations

It may be useful, finally, to ask what has been learned from the experience of the last twenty years. Have any of the lessons we might learn the power to shape the future of curriculum management? Are there any pointers towards what new practices or new theories could look like? The first major reformulation of American government policy in the field of curriculum innovation occurred in 1973. In a widely publicised report to Congress in December 1973, the Central Accounting Office claimed that 200 million dollars invested in the laboratory and research centre structure had produced fewer programmes than expected, that these were poorly evaluated before being disseminated, and that the result was little impact on classroom practice. By this time criticism of the R, D and D models had become intense, and there was a growing body of evidence to suggest that the engineering of educational change on a national scale (even on the 'proliferation of centres' structure which was implemented in the mid-sixties) was not delivering the goods. But even before this damning indictment, and perhaps anticipating it, the Office of Education had set up, in 1972, a new agency to handle its research and development interests. We refer to the National Institute of Education (N.I.E.), which immediately set about the task of reviewing policy in the light of growing dissatisfaction with the inadequacies of established practice. The review, published in 1973, suggested four alterations in the structure for planned educational change:

(1) to develop a monitoring system with N.I.E. to gather and analyse data on the 'knowledge production and utilisation system';
(2) to strengthen the external R and D system;
(3) to build a linkage and support system between the R and D system and school;
(4) to build problem solving capacity into the operating system. (National Institute of Education 1973)

House is unimpressed with the alleged new departures, seeing the shift in direction merely as an attempt to bolster up the old paradigm. *'Plus ça change,'* he laments, predicting that the function of 'support systems' and 'problem solving' will be to open the periphery to the R and D delivery system. He forecasts continuing failure.

On the other hand, these new directions will certainly afford Havelock some satisfaction. We suggested in chapter 1 that his attempt to synthesise the best elements of the three schools of thought was too unselective to offer a practical solution, but clearly the N.I.E. has decided otherwise. It is now embarked on an 'all systems go' policy. We concur with those who define these systems as fundamentally incompatible, and share House's pessimism.

Curriculum reform in England and Wales

But now it is time to turn our attention to the parallel curriculum movement that has been such a striking feature of education in England and Wales since the first 'projects' in science teaching were funded by the Nuffield Foundation in the early sixties.

The wave of criticism which lashed the walls of the American school in the sixties had no real parallel here. No serious educational figure in this country would have described the system in the way Jencks (1963) wrote of the American schools when reviewing the progress of educational reform since Sputnik:

> Yet none of these improvements has appreciably diminished the fundamental parochialism of the majority of schools, the stultifying social standards imposed by the students on one another and tacitly supported by the teachers, the chauvinistic self-congratulatory view of the world conveyed by textbooks and teachers alike, the subordination of education to community solidarity . . . all this and more persists.
>
> (quoted in Miles 1964)

This is the language of confrontation, the bitter, unconditional discourse of battle. British debate about the schools, on the other hand, with few exceptions, is conciliatory if not positively self-congratulatory. To borrow a standard phrase from the pupil report card, 'could do better' is the tone typically struck in this country by curriculum developer and critic alike when referring to the performance of the teaching profession. Yellow press apart (and the London evening papers' sensationalist presentations of the problems of I.L.E.A. schools certainly qualifies them for the label) the discussion of curriculum

31

innovation is generally couched in a judiciously-balanced blend of bouquets and brick-bats, wherein the selected target of criticism, whether it be the schools, the administrators or the teacher educators, usually has its virtues extolled at length before its weaknesses are apologetically pinpointed. Partly of course this is a matter of cultural style. But it is also partly a consequence of the fact that almost all of the participants in the discussion have at one time been schoolteachers, and still remember their own inadequacies and difficulties.

More importantly, we think, the gentleness of the debate reflects a concern to respect the boundaries of curriculum control that have become established. The control of education in this country has been for half a century vested in a delicately balanced tripartite system, with power shared between central government, local government, and teachers (see Jenkins and Shipman 1976, in this series). The most significant and powerful concept underlying this structure is the one that Stuart McLure (1968) alluded to in reporting the Third International Curriculum Conference held one year previously. There is an 'English myth' that the teacher is autonomous in matters of curriculum. McLure continued: 'To refer to this as a myth is not to denigrate it. It is a crucial element in the English educational idea. It is the key to the combination of pedagogic political and administrative initiatives which provide the drive for curriculum reform in England and Wales . . .'

In the debate which preceded and accompanied the setting up in 1964 of the major national agency of curriculum development, the Schools Council, respect for the autonomy of the teacher was declared by all parties; the issue was how the teacher might best be helped fully to exercise that autonomy. No one basically questioned the need for some concerted action. There was a general acceptance, eager in some quarters but grudging in others, that the 'increasing pace of change', the 'knowledge expansion' – especially in science and technology, rising costs, and more extended schooling justified the consideration of new 'machinery' to enable the schools to respond more quickly and more effectively to social change than they had hitherto felt obliged to do. Although there was no consciousness of a 'red menace' to quicken the pulse of action, a far more threatening shadow was already on the teachers' horizon – the raising of the (minimal) school-leaving age from fifteen to sixteen, a change planned to take place in 1970, and belatedly postponed to 1972. Few disputed that the traditional curriculum was unsuited to most of the pupils who left school at fifteen. The programme of innovation that was to cope with the raising of the school-leaving age became known as ROSLA. While the decision to raise the leaving age was hotly criticised by large numbers of teachers, the inevitability of its implementation ensured that the major rhetoric of the Council, 'Preparing for ROSLA', would receive at least a guarded welcome. But of course a consensus on 'need' did not dispose of the matter of instruments, the question of who was going to have responsibility for what.

The pioneer work of the Nuffield Foundation, largely teacher initiated and very much teacher dominated, barely raised a political eyebrow, but the intervention of government was quite a different matter, one which called for scrupulous investigation of the implications, and exhaustive negotiations between the various interested parties. Throughout the fifties, observers of the power-partnership in education had noted signs of increasing 'unrest' within the Ministry about central government's exclusion from the 'secret garden of the curriculum', as Sir David Eccles was to call it caustically in a parliamentary debate on the Crowther Report in 1960. Manzer (1970) describes the period leading up to this comment as one in which the tradition of partnership established between the two world wars was increasingly seen by those in central government as inadequate to the task of efficiently managing an expanding educational system.

Sir David Eccles was the first minister to assume that educational expenditure was economic investment (see Kogan 1974), an equation that found support in the manpower arguments being advanced by sociologists pressing for an end to secondary school selection. In consequence it was under his leadership that the Department moved from its traditional 'regulatory control' role to a positive policy-making role in relation to national goals. The assault on the 'secret garden' was signalled by the setting up in 1962 of a Curriculum Study Group to 'oversee examinations and curriculum'. In view of all the warnings which preceded this central initiative, it is hardly surprising that the reaction of the partners was fast and pretty furious (Nisbet 1973). The upshot of it all was the emergence of the Schools Council with a

33

constitution and terms of reference which were intended to maintain the existing balance of power, and with the principle of teacher autonomy nailed firmly to its masthead. The Schools Council constitution, published each year in its annual report, emphasises that:

> In the execution of this constitution and in the exercise of all functions inferred thereby regard shall at all times be had to the general principle that each school should have the fullest possible measure of responsibility for its own work, with its own curriculum and teaching methods based on the needs of its own pupils and evolved by its own staff.

Caston described the new structure as 'a deliberate resort to democracy' (quoted in Nisbet 1973); Manzer as 'an assertion of orthodoxy and, quite possibly, an opportunity lost' (1970).

Certainly, literal interpretation of the principle of teacher autonomy would virtually invalidate the Council's policy of funding central project teams to generate new teaching programmes, but even the more 'spiritual' interpretation which it adopted entailed severe restrictions upon the kinds of activities it, or its agents, could legitimately engage in. The rhetoric it evolved, in the face of persistent suspicions about its intentions and ambitions, stressed the goal of 'increasing the range of choice available to the teacher', but it has always been evident that the mere provision of choice is insufficient to justify the work and the cost of the Council; unless a great many teachers were persuaded to exercise that choice in favour of the Council's products there wouldn't be much point in its existence. The constitution of the Council was, in that sense at least, a recipe for ambivalence.

The Council's sensitivity to the restrictions in its remit, and its careful avoidance of anything resembling trespass on the territory of other bodies, particularly in the field of teacher training, resulted in a number of first-wave projects feeling that they were unreasonably blocked in their natural aspirations to 'sell' their innovations to the schools. Not that the need to sell was anticipated from the start. Just as in America, the curriculum development was initially imbued with the kind of optimism that Professor Kerr (1967) expressed when he said 'At the practical and organisational levels, the new curricula promise to revolutionise

English education.' It was widely assumed that curriculum innovations would succeed on their self-evident or evaluated merits, and would be gobbled up by the schools.

When it began to be evident, in the late sixties, that it was not going to be as easy as that, projects began to direct some of their energies into plans for dissemination. The concept was, however, a tricky one, susceptible to differing interpretations, only some of which were consistent with the Council's brief and able to command its open support. Dissemination as the promulgation of project developments was blessed; official Council documents made no bones about the need to 'make available information about possible new courses' and 'drawing the attention of those responsible for general arrangements . . . to the implications of their work of new patterns of curriculum, courses and methods'. But those who conceived dissemination as a proselytising activity to be pursued through direct action on the teachers found themselves up against not only the Council constitution but a territorial boundary as well. Teacher training lay outside the jurisdiction of the Council which was, indeed, almost entirely dependent on other agencies for the implementation of innovation. As John Nisbet (1973) observes in his study of the Schools Council, 'Teachers' centres, in-service training and initial training constitute an area where there is a conflict of interests not unlike that which occurred at the formation of the Council. A similar process of negotiation may be necessary to establish a clearer definition of responsibilities.'

Certainly it would have been no easy matter for the Council, or its projects individually, to operationalise a centre-periphery diffusion structure. The regional and local teachers' centres, for instance, which proliferated rapidly with the encouragement of the Council, did not provide the outstations of a radical diffusion process. They were not administratively linked to the Council, nor did the innovation system provide national career structures for the centre leaders (change agents or entrepreneurs). Even within their local power structures many of them were precariously marginal, and caught in the ambiguity of trying to provide an 'uncontaminated' but resource-demanding support service to teachers. Nor did the fact that the L.E.A.s provided half the Council's income stimulate them to create mechanisms for the reception and utilisation of its products. As one chief education officer put it, 'We don't think of it as our money' because we never see it. It's deducted at source'. The L.E.A.s were keen enough to provide participant schools at the development stage of projects, but in the matter of diffusion they were largely content in the early years of the system to endorse the popular view summed up by Shipman (1974): 'Curriculum development was seen as a scattering of seed in the form of projects in hope that the ideas produced would germinate, grow and spread.'

Small wonder that the Council was slow to grasp the nettle of dissemination, especially in the sense defined by the Centre for Educational Research and Innovation – 'Dissemination may be defined as the effective conveyance of a tested innovation as widely as possible within an educational system in such a way that all concerned are encouraged to accept and implement the change.' (O.E.C.D. 1971).

Nevertheless, and however reluctantly, the nettle was grasped and a new phase of 'consolidation', 'improved communication' and finally 'dissemination' began. By this time, about the beginning of the seventies, those critics who had seen the Council as a malignant conspiracy to take over the curriculum had given way to others whose complaint was that it was having no influence on the curriculum at all, and still more who alleged that what they saw in classrooms bore little relationship to the 'package' descriptions of the developers and even less to their proclaimed aspirations. The Humanities Curriculum Project was the first to implement with Council support a systematic programme of dissemination, from 1970 to 1972 (Humble and Simons; Rudduck: both in preparation), but it was the Geography for the Young School Leaver Project, which we shall shortly examine, that gave unprecedented emphasis to this phase of curriculum development and became, in terms of national impact, the jewel in the Council crown.

Current Council policy on dissemination is equivocal. A working party set up in 1972 to consider 'the place of dissemination and in-service training in the work of the Council', delivered a rather tame, though extensive, list of recommendations designed to strengthen rather than change established policy. 'Projects should follow a policy of positive promotion of their ideas and materials' is followed by 'Positive promotion is not the hard sell.' Promotion is apparently confined to creating 'awareness', no more. The working party seems to have an image of projects behaving like wallflowers, too overcome with modesty

36

and shyness to submit themselves to the public gaze. With help, particularly in the form of area information centres, regional project 'consultants' (nice avoidance of politically charged terms like change agent or entrepreneur) and financial support for the production of 'teaching materials for pre-service and in-service course use', they can be helped to overcome these inhibitions. But there is no suggestion that the Council should seek to alter its relationships to other agencies in any structural way, or to change its basic policy. The report concludes:

> We did not feel that any of the problems of dissemination which we have examined were so intractable, in themselves, that they challenged the idea of national curriculum development projects. Nor was it apparent to us that any more local-ised form of curriculum development would avoid these prob-lems, except that by being content to influence the local situa-tion alone, dissemination could be ignored completely.

The report did, however, after endorsing the autonomy of pro-ject directors, recommend a 'firmer relationship' between Council and projects to enable them to 'plan dissemination' to certain defined ends.

The evident reluctance of the working party to recommend a change of course to the Council is understandable in the light of the paucity of hard data available to it about the successes or failures of existing policy. There was a lot of talk, a lot of gloomy foreboding and a general sense of unease, but little more. After all, although the working party conducted its deliberations at a time when the Council was funding more than 160 projects at a cost of six million pounds, only a handful ended before 1971. There was very little evidence, and most of it had been gathered by the Humanities Curriculum Project, from which the Council had virtually severed its relationship. The project was not invited to submit a paper or address the committee, although it was keen to do so.

The working party did, however, have the benefit of a report from Tony Becher, Assistant Director of the Nuffield Founda-tion, on the Foundation's experience in dissemination, and another from Marten Shipman, who for the previous three years had been observing the processes of the Keele Integrated Studies Project.

Becher's analysis was already on record (see Becher 1971). Using Havelock's models, he considered that the first wave of Nuffield projects had employed an R, D and D paradigm, and had been more successful than their American or Swedish counterparts in gaining widespread adoption, averaging round about fifty per cent penetration of the user market within five years of publication, and relying solely on mass publication of teaching packages. However, 'When one looks behind the statistics . . . one finds a surprisingly large variation in the methods of use. Far from "getting the message" implicit in the work of the development team, many teachers have superimposed their own very different interpretations and philosophies.' In particular, these projects had little success in promoting their aims of transforming didactic teaching and passive learning into discovery modes and active pupil participation.

By the mid 1960s, Becher thought, projects, especially primary school projects, were beginning to favour the social-interaction school, with less emphasis on a packaged product, more on the involvement of large numbers of teachers in a process of curriculum reflection which generated source books of ideas. Becher saw this as an inherently weak diffusion model, because the energy and creativity of the primary group of participant teachers was largely a function of their involvement with the central team, and could not be sustained beyond the life of this 'temporary system', or exported. 'An innovation based on social interaction can soon disappear without trace, or survive only in a few odd and isolated mutations.'

Becher's conclusion was that projects which incorporated elements of R, D and D (particularly the production of a course which could be implemented without much effort by the teacher) into a social interaction model stood the best chance of success. Although he still endorsed the idea of a centre-periphery model, he called for more consumer education through in-service training and the use of local school consultants. 'We shall require a very much more effective system of in-service training if educational change is to be, in the future, more than a series of ad hoc adjustments at the periphery of the system, or a series of pious plans at the centre which, even if they do happen to be taken up on a sizeable scale, are often seriously garbled in the process.'

Shipman (1974) was coming to similar conclusions as a result of an intensive study of one Schools Council project.

> The spread of an innovation involves increasing numbers of teachers who lack the skills and the enthusiasm of the pioneers. The promotion prospects of involvement in an innovation are rapidly exhausted and the ambitious look to the next bandwagon. The result is that an apparently successful innovation in the hands of a few can fail when generally adopted and diluted.

In a manner reminiscent of Schon's account of the movement, Shipman described the early Council projects as operating 'in the spaces between national and local agencies responsible for the schools'. He advocated the establishment of an infrastructure which would coordinate national and local efforts, and the expansion of in-service training; and more time for projects (typically funded for three years) to engage in systematic diffusion. Shipman identified the mobility of system personnel at every level as a major source of discontinuity which made reliance on often laboriously built networks of personal contacts very vulnerable. (The Humanities Project also experienced this as a severe problem, and House noted changes of personnel at the 'centre' as a critical cause of breakdown in innovation systems working on a centre-periphery model.)

The working party absorbed these ideas, as well as canvassing views from many other sources. Although their recommendations were seen in many quarters as yet another 'opportunity lost', it must be appreciated that there were strict limits to what they could realistically advocate. The Council was confined by political considerations to a specified territory and a defined role, from which it could not escape without inviting a fundamental reappraisal of the whole innovation system and threatening its own survival. And by this time the 'cooperative machinery' of the Council was firmly in the grip of the teacher unions, whose numerical superiority on Council committees had inevitably led to the exercise of policy control. It was not a position of power they would lightly relinquish. So the working party juggled with the notions of networks and infrastructures, and recommended more information and better communication. Maintaining respect for 'territory', they advocated the installation of more linking agents in the 'no-man's-land' between territories such as field officers and school consultants, and more project courses to 'train trainers' on the Humanities Project model. They could do little more without calling into question the viability of the Council itself.

Concluding comments

In the last twenty years we have witnessed a quite extraordinary effort to industrialise the curriculum of the public schools of America and Britain, and we have seen that effort, in its own terms, fail. It is necessary to say 'in its own terms', because it is too soon to evaluate the impact in terms of its effects. But the objective of short-term transformation of the system has clearly not been met, and both countries are now taking stock.

What has been learned? Perhaps one 'big' lesson. The myth of the 'receiver' has been nailed, and with it the myth of 'dissemination' as the conveyance of a product to a user. Curriculum reform on both sides of the North Atlantic, despite quite fundamental differences in many important respects, was imbued with these myths. Perhaps it still is and the lesson has not been learned. House maintains that the stock-taking in America has yielded merely a change of rhetoric; while the Schools Council still identifies the problem as 'communication' (see next chapter).

Schon says that in a period of rapid social change there must be a developed capacity for 'public learning'. We are now into the second decade of experience of a public policy of curriculum innovation. What, if anything, has been critical in determining the (presumed) failure of policy? We would suggest, speculatively, that one way to understand what has happened is to ask of each innovation system what degree of 'respect' was shown for the established system, its institutions, its processes, its personnel, its achievements? In America, too little. The bombardment of the system in the early sixties was followed by the attempt to 'move in' new institutions, new processes, new personnel with new goals. Such takeover bids for social systems are likely to fail for two reasons: they will be resisted, because they strike at the self-esteem of those they need to co-opt; and the resistance will be successful, because power is much more widely distributed in social systems than those at the centre realise. In this country we have perhaps seen the consequence of too much

40

respect for the established system. The British 'guest' in the social system has as many problems as the American 'gate-crasher'. The 'co-operative machinery' of the Council represents the system, and therefore lacks a mandate to criticise it. It is locked within the protocol of courtesy.

Further reading

As in the previous chapter it is difficult to specify further reading in so condensed a review of a lengthy and complex literature. We do, however, recommend Cremin (1961) on the prehistory of the curriculum reform movement in the U.S.A., Grobman (1970) for systematic information on American projects, and Broudy (1972) for a critical overview of the American scene.

Turning to Britain, the Schools Council (1973) has published a useful survey of projects and Shipman (1974) has given a good historical account of one project in action. Nisbet's study (1973) of the Schools Council itself is particularly recommended as a study of curriculum development at the policy level.

In this brief thumbnail history of the curriculum reform movement we have neglected to mention Scotland, which had an independent tradition of curriculum reform often in advance of England and Wales. Nisbet's survey (1970) redresses the balance on this point.

3 CURRICULUM NEGOTIATION

Initial propositions

> The principal – though by no means the only – target is, of course, the classroom teacher, the 'man at the coal-face'; ensure that the ideas reach him untwisted and still attractive, and the rest of your task is easy. (O.E.C.D. 1971)

This advice is no doubt well-intentioned, and it certainly has an appealing simplicity. But it has little relevance to the real world of the schools, or to the problems of securing change in classrooms. In this chapter we offer our own 'message' about the dissemination of innovation, the process we have characterised as central to systems of planned change. Although the particular focus of the chapter is upon the work of one project, it should not be thought that the phenomena we describe are so confined. We believe that the propositions tentatively advanced and explored in the following pages apply in varying degrees to curriculum development projects generally. The propositions are:

(1) Projects are subordinate to the school system, and can only seek their ends within the limitations and constraints of that system.

(2) Projects engage in image manipulation in order to disguise discrepancies between their own educational convictions and the convictions held by others, particularly teachers on the one hand and academic critics on the other.

(3) There is a consequent generation of two distinct and conflicting views held outside a project concerning what the project essentially 'is'; one view is held by teachers, the other by critics.

(4) The so-called gap between intent and practice is in part a function of the differences between these two views of the project. The gap is therefore partly 'planned'.

(5) The process of curriculum dissemination, in so far as it assumes a stable message, does not occur. The process to which the term 'dissemination' is conventionally applied would be more accurately described by the term 'curriculum negotiation'.

The role of rhetoric

There's a lot to be said for the British tradition of educational rhetoric, a rhetoric which offers an image of the system and all its participants as a 'family firm', driven by shared ideals, all comrades in the common cause of pupil welfare. Images like this can help bring about their own fulfilment, fix aspirations, deflect unwelcome interference and minimise unproductive conflict. In a system so marked as ours is, beneath the shell of complacency that so irritates foreigners, by feelings of failure at all levels of action, the rhetoric of consensus helps to foster the notion that progress, though it may be slow, is certain, and that problems must inevitably surrender to so much co-ordinated goodwill.

Such rhetoric has a useful place. It expresses the public aspirations of the system, and it can help to define the gap between ideals and achievement. But this gap, its extent and its nature, must be kept in clear view, and there is a great deal of evidence to show that, in the curriculum development movement, this gap is sometimes blurred over; the rhetoric and the reality get confused. We treat this issue again in the final chapter. Here we want to focus on one particular product of this confusion – the red herring of the so-called 'communication problem'.

At a recent conference on education, one of the formal sessions was devoted to 'problems of communication'. One of the participants, a senior educational administrator, who had taken upon himself the role of attacking the rhetoric of the conference in each of its focused debates, grew increasingly restive as he listened to successive reiterations of the call for clear and effective communications to reduce the level of misunderstanding and ignorance of the new resources which the curriculum development industry was trying to make available to schools.

At last he broke into the discussion, with an outburst, our recall of which is as follows. The exact words may be awry but the gist is unmistakable: 'If the problem was one of communication, I should long since have been compelled to conclude that the headmasters of my schools are totally incapable of comprehending any message that would tax a backward eight year old child.' The statement having produced its predictable result of temporary disruption and unease, the administrator withdrew into gloomy silence for the remainder of the session, which quickly resumed its flow. Ironically, the reaction of the group to his 'communication' was a prime example of his point. The message was clear, but was not congenial, and was not accepted.

The problem of communication is a product of the rhetoric of curriculum development rather than of the reality. The rhetoric is premised on an unexamined assumption: that all of us concerned with the education of pupils – teachers, administrators, advisers, researchers, theorists – basically share the same educational values and have overlapping visions of curriculum excellence. A confirmation of the argument is the proposition that if there are major discrepancies between the advocacies of the support groups and the behaviour of the practitioner groups, and if these discrepancies cannot be explained in terms of material constraints, then there is prima facie a problem of communication. Both parties conspire in this pretence, and the dreaded 'jargon' is ruthlessly hunted down with all the inquisitorial zeal formerly reserved for witchcraft.

All this is not to say that there are no problems of transmission which can be accounted for in terms of poor presentation: of course there are. But curriculum innovators face a much more significant problem which needs to be distinguished from this but is often confused with it: the issue of whether people want to hear what they have to say. The answer does not necessarily lie in saying it more clearly. On the contrary, the innovator in education often solves his 'communication problems' by altering the content rather than the form of his communication. Paradoxically, we assert, this alteration of the content can be the key to successful dissemination. Havelock (1971) gives us a clue to the social processes underlying this truth: 'Values are the basic stop-and-go signals for human behaviour. Messages which clearly contradict pre-existing values will not get anywhere and those which appeal to them will get far. A perception of shared values will bring resource and user systems together, and perceptions of disparate values will drive them apart.'

We believe this to be true, but quite complex in its implications for curriculum dissemination. It does not follow, for instance, that you cannot successfully disseminate a curriculum whose educational values are not endorsed by those you disseminate it to. This is because the curriculum is always part of a package, not the whole of it. The rest of the package consists of things like membership of the innovating fraternity, occasional release from a boring occupation or a watchful spouse, career qualifications, support for territorial expansion, or defence

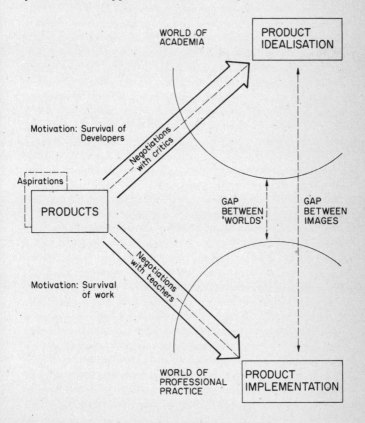

3.1 *Curriculum Negotiation*

against encroachment, devices for attention seeking and attention avoidance, and all the many human purposes that people prosecute with whatever resources come to hand.

Seen from the practitioner's viewpoint the novel curriculum poses a set of pragmatic considerations to do with the task of assimilation, and these may well constitute *prior* rather than *post* considerations. The extent to which an innovation calls upon the innovator to engage the existing institutional context (whether in its administrative, organisational, technical or ethical aspects) in order to secure its implementation, has to be calculated. The unwary seeker after a modest degree of self-improvement has often found himself unwittingly the spearhead of an institutional confrontation he did not aspire to. Similarly, the degree of adaptability to local circumstances and preferences of which the curriculum is capable, the extent to which it is an 'all-or-nothing' challenge or a 'take-what-you-like' assortment, will influence choices. Some observers of the current scene, noting remarkable transformations in the rhetoric of pedagogy but little change in the practice, believe that many have chosen the wrappings, but few the merchandise, of curriculum innovation.

Interpreters of the R, D and D model have widely assumed that the gap between the intents of developers and the realisations of practitioners is explicable in terms of a process of adulteration which begins at the point of entry into the schools and is a result of institutional conservatism compounded by ineptness and indifference on the part of the innovating teachers. Plus, of course, the failures in communication alluded to earlier. Dissemination followed by disintegration. These interpreters are typically academic theorists who have taken the trouble to familiarise themselves with the new curriculum as propounded by the developers in journal articles or at conferences specially held to acquaint the theorist with the concepts, values and practices of the innovation. They have a picture of the curriculum which they then use to evaluate school practice. They assume that the picture they have acquired is the same picture that the practitioner acquired in the course of induction or training for the innovation. It is our purpose in this chapter to contend that in many cases there is a significant discrepancy between these two pictures, a discrepancy which has nothing to do with communication. The gap between the two image-building contexts is depicted, not too fancifully, in Figure 3.1.

Gates and gatekeepers

In this section we want to explore a thesis about curriculum dissemination, a thesis that we have particularly explored and elaborated through observations of a series of conferences involving the Geography for the Young School Leaver project team. The thesis can be simply stated as follows: the gap between project intent and classroom practice is not primarily a matter of miscommunication by the project or misuse by the teachers. Rather it is a consequence of a series of 'trade-offs' that are negotiated at each successive point of sale. 'What is implemented' is much closer to 'what was sold' than is commonly realised. That this truth is not widely understood is due to an idealised image of the new curriculum perpetuated by the self-appointed monitors of curriculum innovation. The relative nature of the perceived truths becomes increasingly clear when we realise that these entrepreneurs are not above the conflict but are themselves openly bidding in the market place where meanings are negotiated. These monitors are usually members of the academic community, whose conception of the project is the product of another 'trade-off' entered into by developers seeking legitimation for their work.

The net effect of these two bargaining processes is to create a significant gap between the critic's image and the practitioner's image of the innovation. Before putting forward the empirical grounds for this thesis, let us first consider whether it is 'plausible'. Are there reasons, circumstances or considerations that might lead us to predict or expect such processes to take place? We think there are, and it may be helpful at this point to draw attention to the constraints unavoidably built into the developer's situation.

It may be useful to ask here to what extent the theories described in chapter 1 might help. Let us consider the curriculum project as the centre of Schon's centre-periphery model. How does it measure up? Very poorly in fact. The truth is almost the reverse of the popular 'bandwagon' image. In terms of permanence and power it is the schools and the L.E.A.s that constitute the centre; projects, and even the Council itself, are marginal, precarious, temporary. The Keele Integrated Studies Project was two people and a secretary in a Nissen hut for three

47

years, the Geography for the Young School Leaver Project one person more in similar quarters. The developers command no one, and can afford to offend very few. They depend entirely upon the voluntary cooperation of system personnel, and have only a short time in which to ensure the survival of their work in schools and to secure their own personal futures.

The development teams themselves are typically drawn from the middle ranks of the academic status structure, unlike American teams, which have been led by university scholars. Project leaders in this country are often college of education lecturers, their development teams seconded teachers of considerable classroom experience and standing. Involvement in project work marks for most of them a point of perceived upward mobility in their career patterns, an opportunity to climb from one level in the system to the next.

John Banks (1968) in his account of the work of the Council up to 1968 says of the project director 'At the end of the road he can console himself that, unless current patterns alter substantially, there is a professorship waiting for him when it's all over.' Earlier in the same account Banks says that the director 'must be able to defend himself against other educationists'. Where the career aspirations of the development team lie within the university sector, their work on the project constitutes their 'credentials'. The 'inspectors' of these credentials may already be members of the universities, either educationists or scholars from the relevant disciplines. Quite often they are, like the project directors, from the middle stratum, the colleges of education, and constitute a 'rival' group, competing for entry to the universities on the basis of their criticism of the developers. (They can also be seen to 'conspire' with developers to create new academic territory.) In this sense the curriculum development movement is a battlefield, with honours pretty well shared over the past decade. Official project evaluators, too, may be staking claims, some choosing to back the project, and even go down with it, others taking up positions nearer to the critics. 'Patterns' have altered. Curriculum theory has quickly become established as an academic subject. Virtually all university departments of education have established courses in curriculum based on the work of Nuffield and the Schools Council, and a growing number of subject departments have introduced an 'educational' element into their structure. In a period of economic recession, with the numbers of university openings dwindling, curriculum developers can make no easy assumptions about their future employment prospects. For almost all of them there is no going back, except as an admission of failure. The experience of project work transforms outlooks and aspirations, even of those who initially expected to go back to the classroom at the end of the project.

What is the nature of the 'examination' that the developers must submit to in pursuit of their personal survival? What constitutes academic respectability? It is dangerous to generalise, but we would suggest that to 'pass the test' the project must evince

(1) a 'non-divisive' view of the curriculum needs of the pupil;
(2) a high estimate of the ability of the low-achieving pupil;
(3) a fully articulated theory of pedagogy in its content area;
(4) a new curriculum that embodies the 'latest' conception of the subject held by university scholars.

The first two of these conditions are strongly held values within the education departments of universities and colleges of education, and bulwarks of the ideology of educational sociologists, who in this country have exerted a strong critical influence since the late fifties. The third condition is a 'requirement' of the philosophers of education, whose influence, particularly in the teacher training sector, is still very powerful, and the fourth condition emanates from those subject specialists who are generally prominent in the period leading up to the launching of the innovation and who continue to take a close interest in it.

At this point it may be worth pausing to remind the reader that project team members are themselves likely to share these values anyway. Curriculum reform attracts optimistic progressives, if not visionaries, and sponsors look for people who seem to represent the growth-points in the field. There is rarely any hypocrisy involved in matching the values of the academic critics.

But the developers also have another audience whose values and expectations have to be engaged if the products of their work are to make their way in the system, and they are only too well aware that the critics have the advantage of being able to shift their attack to failures of implementation. The first wave of Nuffield Science developers were fortunate in being largely free from the now intense pressure on developers to demonstrate effective-

49

ness in terms of widespread adoption of new programmes (see chapter 4). The Geography for the Young School Leaver project on the other hand was funded at a point of acute disquiet about the cost-effectiveness of the large project, following the report of a Council-organised conference in 1969 which 'saw an urgent need for re-examination' of diffusion. The survival of the Council itself was beginning to be seen as an issue, one which demanded improved performance in the market place. The project team, thinking independently, met this need with a systematic and well-organised plan. But how could any plan succeed to the extent that the Geography project has (33 per cent adoption in fifteen months)? What are the conditions of mass teacher acceptability, and how do they compare with the conditions of academic respectability that we have identified? Again it is dangerous to generalise, but we would suggest that large scale acceptance depends on teachers perceiving the project as

(1) offering solutions tailored to the less able adolescent;
(2) based on a 'realistic' view of the limitations of the pupil;
(3) respecting their 'autonomy' with regard to classroom practice;
(4) offering reinforcement to their professional identity.

We can see in these delineations of the value systems of the project's two major audiences a potential difficulty for the developers who seek both academic legitimation and large scale sales. The difficulty is compounded by the constraints which arise from the project's role as an agent of the Council. There must be sales, but no 'sell'. The teacher's autonomy is sacrosanct. He already knows 'how to teach'. But, as Stenhouse (1975) has said, curriculum development depends crucially upon changing the skills of the teacher. His own highly original solution to the problem in the Humanities Project (and we must stress that there is no imputation of calculated intent) was to offer a fully articulated pedagogy under the guise of a research instrument for the teacher, thus gaining both a penetrative purchase on classroom practice and academic respectability at the same time.

Given these sets of conflicting constraints, we think our thesis has prima facie plausibility. We now try to sketch the empirical data which generated the thesis. The remaining major sections of this chapter bring focus to our search for evidence in support of the propositions advanced. In sequence we shall be conside-

ring
  (a) A project profile of G.Y.S.L.;
  (b) The dissemination of G.Y.S.L.;
  (c) Concluding comments: images of G.Y.S.L. In this final
       section we return to the theoretical frameworks and try to
       assess the extent to which the analysis bears them out.

A project profile of G.Y.S.L.

The purpose of this project profile is to present summarising
information that hopefully adds up towards a pen-portrayal of
the project. The portrayal includes a selection of basic facts as
well as an element of interpretation.

Geography for the Young School Leaver Project
  Time scale: 1970-76 (1970-3 in the first instance)
  Total Grant: approximately £100,000
  Remit: 'to examine the contribution that geography can make
  to the education of average and below average pupils between
  the ages of 14 and 16 and to produce schemes of work and
  supporting resources that can be used either in a subject or
  interdisciplinary framework.'
  Project team: four people, two of them part-time
    (1) and (2) Rex Beddis and Tom Dalton, half-time co-
        directors, both senior lecturers in geography at Avery
        Hill College of Education in London
    (3) Trevor Higginbottom, full-time research assistant, sec-
        onded head of the geography department of a
        comprehensive school in Sheffield
    (4) Pamela Bowen, full-time research assistant, formerly a
        geography teacher in the Inner London Education
        Authority
  Location: an ad hoc centre in Avery Hill College.
  Materials: Three theme-based kits have been produced and
  published. Each consists of resource items mainly collected on
  a case study basis and organised into teaching units. Film
  strips and audiotapes are included. The Teacher's Guide consists of one copy of every item in the kits except the audio-
  visual materials. It offers for each unit a list of objectives,
  resources and teaching procedures.

51

Sales (figures up to September 1975)

	Kits	Teacher's guide
Theme 1: Man, Land and Leisure (May 1974)	1,500	3,600
Theme 2: Cities and People (October 1974)	1,300	3,200
Theme 3: People, Place and Work (May 1975)	700	1,500

Publishers: Nelson

Prices: Kit just under £50; Teacher's Guide £5

School Participation:

1970-71 (feasibility trials): five schools in South-East London

1972-73 (main trial): twenty-three schools in five regional groups, plus twenty-two associate schools

Extensions:

(1) 1973-74: full team continued, for materials editing and diffusion

(2) Trevor Higginbottom continued, as national coordinator of the dissemination programme

(3) 1975-76: Higginbottom continued, as full-time co-ordinator

During the project's trial phase the team worked in pairs allocated on a regional basis, and made frequent visits both to schools and to regional group meetings. The regional groups then provided the basis for the project's dissemination.

Project strategy

Project strategy is complex. Although the project is sometimes depicted as a 'materials production' enterprise the team reject this interpretation and speak in terms of a three-fold strategy in which materials production is only one element. Put crudely, the materials ensure dissemination but the local groups ensure implementation. Trevor Higginbottom (1975) outlines the elements of project strategy as follows:

After lengthy discussions with both teachers and L.E.A. representatives the project adopted a three-fold strategy for dissemination and implementation.

(a) The publication of exemplar teaching material relating to three main themes: Man, Land and Leisure; Cities and People; and People, Place and Work. This material would illustrate the project's philosophy, provide a catalyst in the continuing debate concerning the contribution of geography to the curriculum and give what many teachers suggested was much needed support in the classroom.

(b) The creation of local curriculum groups in every L.E.A. to establish a collaborative framework for teachers wishing to implement the project's work. In the long term it was hoped that each group would focus on the following activities:

the preparation of local resources – maps, air photographs, statistics, local newspaper articles, etc. – on issues analogous to those in the project's themes;

the preparation of alternative case studies which might afford contrast or greater immediate relevance to pupils in their particular area (e.g. most accessible national park, new town, urban motorway, industrial estate, etc.);

the planning and development of further curriculum units;

an exchange of ideas on the various ways in which the project may be implemented in school – types of organisational framework, syllabuses, styles of assessment, etc.;

participation in an advisory team to assist other teachers in the local authority willing to develop the project's style of work.

Each group would be led by a local coordinator, and a team of regional coordinators would be appointed in an attempt to ensure that there would be inter-L.E.A. collaboration at the regional level. One member of the central team would remain at the Project Centre to act as national coordinator for the programme.

(c) Close collaboration would be established with the external examination boards to try to ensure that those schools wishing to incorporate the project into an examination framework would be sympathetically supported.

Background

In 1961 the American High School Geography Project began, under the auspices of the Joint Committee on Education of the Association of American Geographers and the National Council for Geographic Education. During the following decade it attempted to redefine geography teaching in the light of the revolutionary changes in the discipline which had taken place since the end of the second world war. The overall trend of these changes was to push geography nearer to the conceptual structures and techniques of a social science, with an increasing emphasis on quantitative methods, prediction and generalisation. There was also a growing preoccupation with social and political processes. A similar process of redefinition was going on in Britain too over the same period. The Madingley seminars of the sixties brought together geography teachers anxious to pin down the 'new geography' and analyse its implications for teaching. During the sixties there were some piecemeal changes of practice in individual classrooms, some of them involving adaptations of the work of the American project, but it was not until the end of the decade that the 'movement' generated enough impetus to lead to the funding of two geography projects for secondary schools, Geography 14-18 and the Geography for the Young School Leaver project.

At a conference for innovating geographers held in 1970, a university geographer summarised the new developments and abstracted five possible implications for the future direction of school work:

(1) A move from a factually-based to a concept-based mode of study.
(2) A move from regional to systematic work.
(3) A move from compartmentalised to interdisciplinary work.
(4) A move from qualitative to quantitative statements.
(5) A move from a lesser to a greater emphasis on values.
                                    (Ambrose, in Walford 1973)

At the same conference was Rex Beddis, soon to be invited to co-direct one of the new projects. Beddis outlined his commitment to a subject-based curriculum grounded in the key ideas of the discipline: 'If we are to have a subject-based curriculum then we must do what this implies – teach geography. And that means teaching geographical ideas . . . The content of our geography courses should be not facts, nor techniques, but geographical ideas' (Beddis, in Walford 1973). Beddis thought the time was ripe: 'Many teachers have for a long time been unhappy about the rapidly increasing body of facts they felt obliged to teach, the sterile and unstimulating nature of the learning asked of pupils, and the naive and trivial explaining involved.' Were the pupils capable? 'It is nonsense to suggest that we must not allow people

54

to think until they reach a certain point in their school lives – no concepts before A level . . . Pupils who are made to think about geographical ideas and related themes are being more effectively prepared for an adult role in a rapidly changing society . . .' And a concept structure made possible a non-divisive curriculum: 'Whatever content is chosen, this common core for all abilities is vitally necessary if non-streaming and the comprehensive need for mobility are to be anything other than shams.'

Project philosophy
Geography is 'essentially concerned with spatial patterns and the processes that shape them' (Beddis 1972). 'More and more geography teachers have come to regard the crucial part of their work to be the introduction of the ideas and theories of geographers rather than the mere description of places' (Beddis 1973).

The key element in the project approach is to move geography out of a 'capes-and-bays' tradition into the study of complex social geographical issues which will help pupils to understand their society and to 'make judgements about alternative courses of action both as individuals and as members of a democratic society.' The pedagogic goal could be summarised as 'concept-based understanding of spatial relationships'.

The materials developed were theme-based. Within each theme the team employed a loose 'engineering' model of curriculum design, with objectives clustered in three groups – ideas; skills; values and attitudes.

Dissemination
More successfully than any previous project, the central team built up a national network of 'secondary centres'. Of the 104 new L.E.A.s, 102 now give some support to the project in terms of nominating a local coordinator and making some financial commitment to the purchase of materials. Support is variable, from two-days-per-week-release of a coordinator and full subsidy of all schools wishing to acquire the kits, to very modest assistance to enable meetings between local teacher participants. Most local coordinators are involved in the production and distribution of local resource materials, and in holding dissemination meetings to extend local participation.

There are twelve regional coordinators, most of whom are college of education lecturers. Local coordinators are advisers, college lecturers, teachers'centre wardens, or teachers. The full-time national coordinator is Trevor Higginbottom. There are regular meetings between coordinators, and occasional ones between regional coordinators. The flow of information and ideas throughout the network is maintained by Higginbottom via visits, phone calls, correspondence and the circulation of centrally, regionally and locally produced news bulletins.

Adoption
According to Nelson's sales figures, G.Y.S.L. has penetrated 33 per cent of the market (on sales of kits alone) in only fifteen months. This is a quite unprecedented rate of adoption, and at a time when the schools are alleged to be 'tired of innovation' and L.E.A.s 'disillusioned' about curriculum development projects.

(b) The dissemination of G.Y.S.L.

More than any other British curriculum project dissemination has been planned as a major feature of G.Y.S.L. from the inception of the project. In 1973-4 the full team was engaged virtually full-time in running regional conferences and in supporting the emerging local groups. During 1973 all L.E.A.s were asked if they would support the project by appointing a local coordinator and sending a team of teachers to a regional conference. Administratively this was complicated by the fact that most L.E.A.s were planning for local government reorganisation, which was due to take effect in the middle of G.Y.S.L.'s regional conference programme. Nevertheless, the project received a favourable initial response. Before the regional conference programme began, over seventy of the 104 'new' L.E.A.s had given some support, and by the end of the year this figure had grown to a hundred.

Whether we look at the project from the point of view of its sales, the extent of its adoption at L.E.A. level, or the degree and extent of support given to local groups, it is clear that G.Y.S.L. had been unusually successful in securing some degree of implantation in the system. This degree of success merits a full analysis of the project's dissemination strategy, both at the levels of plans and at the level of action. We do not have the space to give such a full analysis here, and to attempt it is in some ways

56

premature, for as we write one member of the project team is still continuing as full-time national coordinator of G.Y.S.L.

What we would like to do is to look at one problem that faces any large scale and successful dissemination strategy, the problem we raised at the start of this chapter of how a project manages to reconcile the demands of conflicting audiences. The problem is real for the project. One of the project team members commented about the diagram on p. 45 that it vividly captured what he felt was a key feature of dissemination in action. He felt himself to be caught between the two audiences, and when he stood up to address a meeting, or went to talk to key individuals in an L.E.A. or an examination board, he had to judge his presentation quickly and accurately.

We stress that this does not mean that the project team gives different accounts of itself to different audiences. As we shall see, what is said to different audiences by G.Y.S.L. has been highly consistent. Furthermore the team claim that throughout the development and dissemination of the project they have had no real fundamental differences of opinion or conflicts of values. Our observations support this claim, and indeed it is unlikely that the project would have been so productive if the team had been seriously engaged in internal warfare. In talking about responding to different audiences when presenting the project we are not talking about the intentional communication of alternative messages, but about more subtle shades of meaning that stem from different ways of sequencing, emphasising, or editing what is said. What is significant is often what is not said, rather than what is.

We want to attempt to illustrate this theme by looking briefly at two G.Y.S.L. project conferences. One was a regional training conference – one of the eleven conferences in the 1973-4 dissemination programme. The other was a conference held in September 1974 at a Cambridge college, and was intended to be a 'critical appraisal' of the project by a mainly academic audience. As we shall see, the presentation of the project was consistent. Essentially the same things were said at each conference. But also we hope to show that there were differences in the image of the project at each conference which arose from differences in sequencing, emphasis and style of presentation. Often these differences derived from quite subtle and apparently irrelevant items. For example, one team member described to us how, as he

57

left home on the first morning of the Regional Training Conference, he decided at the last minute that what he was wearing was inappropriate. He took off a dark brown cord, safari-style jacket and replaced it with a rather more worn tweed jacket. Not fully conscious of his reasons for doing this, he nevertheless felt more comfortable in front of an audience of teachers with his less stylish jacket (Lawrence Stenhouse has used the phrase 'educated intuition' to describe this situational responsiveness). Perhaps in this instance his sensitivity was compounded by the recognition that the audience he would face included former colleagues, who no doubt would see him first as a teacher and only second as a project team member.

Our claim that projects manipulate their images in response to their perceptions of the expectations of different audiences rests on evidence at this level of subtlety. Inevitably what we are talking about is the project-as-presented-by-its-advocates rather than the project as a disembodied pack of materials. Indeed it is very difficult for us to demonstrate what we mean without entering into some portrayal of the team-member-as-representative-of-the-project. Our belief is that on first contact with the project at a meeting or conference, much of the initial impression we get of the project is inextricably linked with our impressions of the person who represents the project. What we judge, almost intuitively, is the worth of the person. Unconsciously the questions we ask ourselves are like the questions we ask ourselves of the politician who wants our vote. Does this person recognise my situation, predicament, style of life? What are his motives in wanting my support? Can I trust him?

No doubt we have overstated the case, but curriculum developers themselves recognise the structure of the situation. The ambitious dissemination plans of the Geography team's strategy has meant that they have dealt extensively in establishing relationships at school and L.E.A. levels, based on brief and often formalised encounters. The intricate national, regional and local network they have created is sustained by such relationships and such encounters. Inevitably, though not necessarily consciously, they have become sensitive to impression management and socially skilled at negotiation; and recognise the qualities, in themselves and others, that we usually ascribe to 'personality'.

G.Y.S.L. presents itself to two conferences

In this section we want to illustrate our general thesis, bearing in mind the qualifying statements we have just made about the degree of subtlety involved in image manipulation. First we shall look at a conference organised by the project for teachers – the Regional Conference. Second we shall look at a conference organised by the Cambridge Institute of Education for a more general audience – the Cambridge Conference.

1 *The Regional Conference*

Context

This conference was one of eleven held between October 1973 and May 1974 in order to disseminate G.Y.S.L. nationally and to gain continued support for the project within the L.E.A.s after the demise of the central project team during 1974.

The Regional Project Conferences were each located in an area that had been involved in the project's trial phase. During development the project had initiated out-of-school meetings for trial school teachers which were intended to form the nucleus for the later development of local groups. The Regional Project Conference thus marked a point of expansion and dispersal of these initial groups.

During the project's trial phase the four project team members had worked in pairs in supporting the schools and beginning to establish local groups. The team continued this pattern in staffing the Regional Conferences, so that each conference was staffed by two team members.

What did the project team intend to communicate?

The project team saw the main task of the Regional Conferences as one of ensuring widespread adoption in the schools and strengthening the support given by L.E.A.s to the local groups. To put it crudely, it was a selling exercise. The team was obviously anxious to sell the ideas of the project and gain a commitment to its work; at times it was difficult not to appear to be selling the kits commercially as well. The presence one evening of a strong contingent from the publisher emphasised this, and at times during the conference the project team betrayed some embarrassment at being put in the role of salesmen, seemingly going out of their way to distance themselves from the publishing enterprise and attempting to raise wide issues of project philosophy.

That the conference was seen as potentially a sales conference was inevitable, given that the central problem for the project team, at this stage in the dissemination programme, was to ensure widespread adoption. In order to sustain the local groups it was important to ensure widespread and rapid uptake of the project. This was made feasible by the fact that materials were being made available to schools during the year in which the Regional Conferences were being held.

We stress this point in order to emphasise that the Regional Conferences represented a point in the project where the team were under maximum pressure to 'sell' the project to teachers. They were talking to audiences *they* had convened (albeit indirectly), and whom they saw as the leading edge of project progress. More than at any other stage in the project these conferences marked a point where the team had to communicate the project to an audience of teachers whose commitment was uneven and who apparently had little to gain in extrinsic rewards.

What was said at the conference?

The conference programme involved a range of activities, including simulation exercises, a field trip, and lectures from visiting speakers. Predominantly though it consisted of (often alternating) lectures and discussion groups.

In this account we are primarily concerned with the way in which the project team presented the project, so we focus on sessions in which team members formally addressed the whole conference. Since we have emphasised the critical nature of first impressions, we look more closely at the early part of the conference than at the closing sessions.

From the argument so far it will be clear that it is very difficult for us to make our point without describing the events of the conference, and the presentations given by the project members, in some detail. The points we wish to make relate to an argument which is generally applicable, but they are difficult to substantiate without recourse to description which is both specific and personal. We are anxious that the accounts that follow should be seen in terms of qualities of situations and not as critical of persons. Consequently the style we have adopted is somewhat awkward in that it attempts to depersonalise descriptions while recognising the impact and importance of individual qualities. While the style may be awkward it is perhaps necessary, for it protects us from over-personalising the *argument*, which essentially concerns the social nature of human communication and the significance of the structural features of the situations within which communication occurs.

First impressions 1

Both the conferences we shall describe opened with very similar statements of project design and philosophy. These pointed to three general themes.

First, the notion of 'The Young School Leaver': 'Does the project title', the speaker asked, 'and the Schools Council sponsorship of another project [the Bristol-based Geography 14–18 Project aimed at 'O' level pupils] mean that the Schools Council is sponsoring two kinds of knowledge for different levels of ability?' The answer the project gave was 'No: geography is concerned with the deep issues in society and these are essentially nondivisive.' The project argued for a core curriculum with a common structure of concepts. Despite the title of the project, G.Y.S.L. was concerned with a special curriculum for the less able only in terms of techniques of presentation, not in terms of course content.

Second, the theme of curriculum planning was introduced. 'What are we about?' the speaker asked. The answer, for G.Y.S.L., was 'We want to enable pupils to cope with life in its full sense.' But it was important to translate such aims into the kind of behaviour you were aiming for, and later the lecture went on to detail an objectives cycle of curriculum development which proceeded from objectives to resources, to procedures, to assessment and finally back to objectives.

Geography as a discipline was introduced as a major theme. The project team stressed the discipline because they felt that the curriculum, while relating to pupils' needs and interests, also requires the progression and breadth which a discipline can provide. The speaker raised the question of changes in the discipline, seeing the 'new geography' as a shift from the physical to the social environment, towards urban man, a shift towards quantification and model-building, a shift away from the notion of uniqueness to the notion of recurrence, a shift to hypothesis testing and to links with other disciplines. As a project whose audience is the young school leaver, how far could they reflect these changes in the discipline?

The lecture was very professionally delivered. The style was formal and the delivery even and fluent; the tone was quietly assured and emphatic. It was listened to attentively throughout. There were no questions and no interruptions.

OUR COMMENTS (1) The issue of objectives was discussed at some length with only minimal use of the theoretical language associated with the objectives model of curriculum design. The lecture avoided jargon and made only brief references to theorists, and then only for clarification and support (Peters once on 'aims'; Bruner once on the notion of 'core concepts'; Taba twice on 'objectives').

(2) The model presented was a simplified one and presented as if it were uncontroversial and easy to use.

(3) In outlining the project's guidelines for theme selection and development the speaker omitted one of the principles included in the Teacher's Guide. The four principles he detailed were:

(i)   the work should be concerned with all aspects of pupil development including ideas, facts, attitudes and skills;
(ii) the theme should be of interest and relevance to pupils now, but should also have long-term significance;
(iii) there should be a structure of ideas which focuses attention on the concepts of the discipline;
(iv) the method should include full pupil involvement and participation.

The fifth principle (included in the Teacher's Guide) is that 'all pupils, irrespective of ability, should be given the opportunity to explore similar basic ideas at different levels of sophistication.'

First impressions 2

After lunch on the first day of the conference we were given another view of the project, when a member of the project team attempted to translate the picture we had been given of project philosophy into classroom practice. The speaker stated the aim of the lecture clearly. 'This morning we were given a broad view of the project, but now we must approach the chalk-face: get down to the nitty gritty. We have an approach in terms of aims and objectives, but objectives are only the coathangers on which lessons are built. The problem for us is: What are we going to do when we face 4Z on Monday morning?'

'What are we going to do when we face 4Z on Monday morning?' The question seemed to bring the conference to life. The audience seemed suddenly disturbed from its quiet repose.

The phrase '4Z' was destined to become something of a keynote phrase for the rest of the week, constantly recurring informally and in the discussion groups. The project team's use of it early in the conference seemed to mark a point of mutual recognition between project team and audience.

The speaker admitted that when he had been a teacher he hadn't given much attention to working out his objectives. But the project felt that geography teachers still put a lot of emphasis on factual learning and while they did not dispute the need for pupils to acquire facts, they felt the time had come to place more emphasis on ideas. The experience of the trial school teachers was that the working out of objectives was one way this could be accomplished.

The speaker went on to talk about attitude objectives. The project's aim was not to inculcate middle-class values, or to shift geography away from cognitive concerns, but for pupils to consider their own attitudes to the ideas and issues raised. He added: 'But it is important to remember 4Z, and it is up to each teacher to modify all the project's suggestions in the light of what they felt was possible with 4Z'.

Later that day three of the project's trial school teachers talked about their experiences in using project materials, each reinforcing the image of 'teaching 4Z' which had by then become shorthand within the conference. All three came over as serious, competent and hard working, giving detailed accounts of the work they had done with the trial version of the Man, Land and Leisure kit, and presenting an image of 4Z as less able almost to the point of handicap (unable to read newspaper articles, to write more than a few lines, to follow instructions on a work-sheet, to read a map, to be allowed out of school unescorted . . .).

This conflicted somewhat with some of the work which was on display, by children from one of the schools, since this seemed careful, painstaking and at times quite difficult. One teacher confessed to some of us who asked about this afterwards that he was worried at the response he might get at the conference from 'some of the grammar school teachers'.

Another teacher told the conference how he had succeeded in organising a survey of local leisure facilities. The survey was described in great detail and had culminated in the class taking a vote on which of three villages in the school catchment area was most favourably located. The teacher confessed to 'fiddling the vote' so that they got the right answer, but asserted that 'at least voting had given them a sense of involvement in a democratic process.' He closed his account with the story of one of his pupils who had later been in court on a charge of vandalism. 'When I asked him why he'd done it, he said "What do you expect? I've nowhere to play!" '

OUR COMMENTS   (1) This really was Geography for the Young School Leaver. The emphasis throughout was on 4Z.

(2) The main continuity with the first presentation was in the selling of the objectives model which was reinforced virtually in the same words.

First impressions 3

On the third day of the conference the project team showed a videotape made in one of the trial schools. The tape showed one teacher and one class doing field studies within the Man, Land and Leisure theme. After some discussion of this, one of the project team went on to outline Cities and People and to describe how fieldwork could be carried out in the urban environment.

The materials for Cities and People include four case studies of contrasting urban residential areas. The speaker suggested these could be used as a basis for conducting similar studies in the immediate school neighbourhood, and perhaps later in more distant areas of the town or city. The aim was to combine the published case studies with local first hand studies, forming hypotheses in one and testing them against the other.

At this point the speaker switched into anecdote. 'I gave a lecture in Hull recently where I described the studies of residential patterns in different areas of the city done by one school. Someone stood up and said, "This is definitely the work of the Left; the Geography for the Young School Leaver Project are the reds under the Schools Council bed. You've no business to be stressing the differences between residential areas." Well,' sighed the speaker, 'I suppose that's a view he holds.'

Later the speaker returned to the same theme but from an alternative viewpoint. 'Could this be an education in frustration we are providing? – simply revealing inequalities but offering no remedies. After all 80 per cent of our kids are from the working class – whatever that might be' he added rather hastily, but then continued 'I sometimes think that as teachers we're all working class.'

'Should these local studies lead to participation? Does it mean inviting planners into the classroom? Does it mean doing something about these things, getting involved in conservation issues, planting trees perhaps? Is tree planting a suitable activity for 4Z? Are we talking about education or about power? What happens if the kids get involved? Just what is the school's role in society? At what point does the school stop?' The speaker paused. 'I raise these as vital questions for geography teachers to consider.'

OUR COMMENTS   This stress on the political issues raised by the project was not significantly picked up by the teachers either informally or in discussion groups. Some were noticeably disturbed by it, including one of the trial school teachers who dissociated himself from the central team with the comment: 'I'm a geography teacher, that's all.'

Summary

The Regional Conference opened with a clear, even-toned statement of project philosophy, design and intent. In the sessions that followed, this was modified by two statements that were consistent with the initial statement but which elaborated particular meanings. The first was a clear recognition of and identification with the teachers of '4Z'. The second was a statement of political commitment. The first qualifying statement was clearly communicated to the audience; our impression was that the second statement was not.

Context

In September 1974, the Cambridge Institute organised a conference with the aim of undertaking a critical analysis of G.Y.S.L.
This was intended to be the first of a series of conferences, each of
which would focus upon a specific curriculum development project. (Plans for further conferences were in fact shelved when the
organiser, Hugh Sockett, a philosopher of curriculum, was
appointed to the chair of education at the New University of
Ulster.) The agenda of the conference included addresses from
the central project team and from teachers of the project, and
evaluations of its work from Denis Lawton of London University
and from three Cambridge lecturers, Rex Walford, a geographer, John Murrell, a psychologist, and Rex Gibson, a
sociologist, together with an account of a Project Regional
Conference by the two authors of this book.

The conference was organised with the full assent and
cooperation of the project team, and was intended to concentrate on a critical perspective. Unfortunately for the coherence of
the conference, almost half the people who came were geography
teachers looking for an 'induction' course, and the conference as
planned had too little information input to prevent the teachers
becoming rather frustrated before very long. Eventually, the
conference split into two groups, one following its planned
course, while the other was taken through an abbreviated
introduction. Our interest here is in the interaction between the
project team and the evaluators.

First impressions 1

The opening statement was very similar to that given at the Regional Conference. Reflective in tone and wide in perspective, it
located the project within an historical framework of curriculum
development and educational change. The speaker talked about
the project title and explained that in the title and their remit
there were certain restrictions they were anxious to escape. The
spread of comprehensivisation, the growth of mixed ability
teaching, the development of a 'common culture', all marked
changes in the schools that were entirely consistent with the
wide applicability of the project's ideas and materials. But there
was a danger of over-specification by a project team, leading to

arrested development. The important thing was to make sure that the 'deeper messages' of the project were communicated, messages about the implications of change and the need for experimental approaches in the classroom. Kenneth Richmond was quoted to the effect that there was a great deal of inertia in the system, and that perhaps the curriculum couldn't be changed without changing the whole system.

Following this introduction the speaker went on to describe the classic curriculum planning model, the 'objectives model', and how the team had used it to build their materials and were recommending it to adopting teachers. Acknowledging, at various points, the controversiality of the approach through objectives, the speaker justified their use of it in a simplified form. The presentation ended by emphasising the project team's commitment to a common course for all pupils, 'irrespective of ability'.

First impressions 2

Remember that in the Regional Conference the opening statement of project philosophy and design was followed by a qualifying statement that strongly featured 4Z. At the Cambridge Conference, however, the major qualifying statement took a different form, raising a set of 'critical choice' issues where the project's decisions needed to be justified. Among the questions raised were the following. Was the project's adoption of a concept-based geography right, and had the project introduced the main concepts? Was it too parochial, with its emphasis on local studies? The project advocated involvement in the local environment, hoping to change it. Was this justified? Were the team imposing middle-class values on the kids through this curriculum? Could this curriculum appeal to all ability levels or was it too babyish? What about sociology? Increasingly they felt this curriculum was leading to a form of political education. Had they taken too strong a line on this or not faced it? What about dissemination and implementation? Had they assessed the problems correctly, or should assessment come from the grass roots? Were published packages inhibiting or facilitating? And what about the implications of the project for the teacher – a different style of pedagogy, resource management, collaboration with other disciplines, involvement in the affective domain, uncertainty, hard work, frustration. Was it all worth it?

These questions were thrown out in rapid succession. The

delivery was stimulating, conveying as it did an impression of a project that was its own sternest critic, a project whose radical (in broad educational terms) leanings were tempered by a stern regard for propriety of action. In effect, the delivery was in the nature of a pre-emptive strike, drawing much of the expected sting from the critics' tails.

Cambridge: the critics' response

As it turned out, the 'critics' were in general much impressed by the project, and prepared to endorse what they perceived to be the values and educational philosophy of the team. But the conditions of endorsement were made manifestly clear by each speaker, and it is worth our while to illustrate what these conditions were. Let us take two instances, the commentaries of the geographer Rex Walford and of the sociologist Rex Gibson. (Both were kind enough to make printed versions of their talks available to us after the conference.)

Walford was concerned to reassure himself on two issues in the project. The first was very straightforward and the answer clear. The project 'relegates factual information to an adjunctive role in its objectives'. Had it not done so, he warned, 'it would have been paramount to a declaration of intellectual bankruptcy'. Walford's second question was about the conceptual structure of the new geography in the project, and on this question he was less clear. Having examined the project materials thoroughly, he was not satisfied that it had operationalised its Brunerian commitment to dealing with the key ideas of the discipline. Rather, he considered that it tended to deal in 'second-order' concepts and 'only hint at the first-order concepts that lie behind these'. Nor did he feel that the project had achieved a conceptual 'structure', but had settled for 'lists' of concepts without linkage. He warned of the possible consequences of this: 'I fear that without clear identification of first-order concepts and structures of ideas the chances are increased that the *content* of the themes will rise to the surface of the minds of those who examine the materials in relation to teaching and learning.' He exhorted the project team 'not only to espouse the priority of ideas, but to proselytise that view on every available opportunity, if its intentions are not to be misunderstood, or translated back into content perspectives'.

Rex Gibson was also worried about the possibility of unintended and undesirable effects of the project, although he was happy with its aspirations. 'It is the raising of the school leaving age which gives the opportunity for the project to achieve what I think is the objective of its directors: to provide a genuinely common course for the whole range of the fourteen- to sixteen-year-old group, irrespective of ability or attitudes or motivation . . .' The danger lay in possible misuse: 'If G.Y.S.L. is confined to this group (ROSLA) they will be reinforced in their separateness: the social category which will come increasingly to have most significance for them will be the simple one of desire to leave school.' Gibson welcomed the project's implications for interdisciplinary work: 'There is a plain need for integration – for working together with social scientists . . . what is implied is some form of political education.' But what the project was advocating 'puts into question traditional assumptions not only about the nature of geography, but about the nature of professional identity'. This was a threat the teachers would have to cope with in a transition to a new role.

Gibson's major criticism of the project was directed at what he called its 'consensual' view of society. 'The project is rooted in a particular model of society held (consciously or unconsciously) by the project team . . . it is basically consensual . . . seen in its heavy emphasis on "planning" . . . the tacit assumption that agreement can be reached between conflicting interests.' This constitutes 'an underplaying of the importance of power as a fact of life'. Gibson ended by advocating a much more positive pursuit of value objectives in relation to the social issues which the project raised in the classroom. 'Our whole culture or style of life is less rich (i.e. less shapely and various) and is less strong (i.e. less adaptable to changes of circumstance) if people of any age group believe that they should not or cannot influence authority.'

It is not our purpose here to debate the validity of these views, but rather to use them to illustrate the nature of the values and expectations to which the project is exposed, and to indicate the kind of image of itself which it conveys to such an audience.

Concluding comments

We have described the presentations given by G.Y.S.L. to two different audiences: teachers at a regional conference and academic critics at Cambridge. The central account the project gives of itself is consistent, but the project qualifies this account in two different ways. At the Regional Conference the account is qualified by the notion of 4Z and (less successfully) by a plea for a more conscious consideration by the geography teacher of the school's role in society. At Cambridge the account is qualified by a thorough intellectual self-analysis.

In this discrepancy there is no suggestion of dishonesty. The project is merely trying to engage two different audiences. In one situation it uses one set of arguments, in another situation a different, but quite compatible set.

Yet it is from this kind of selective responsiveness to the interests of different audiences that different images of the project evolve. This is very clear in the case of the Keele Integrated Studies Project where different notions of the nature of 'integration' came from the different affiliations of different kinds of team members.

The Keele project was set up initially to examine the problems and possibilities of an integrated approach to humanities teaching in secondary schools. Central to its remit was the rather complex problem of the conceptualisation of what was to count as integration. The problem of the two audiences was clearly visible in the different accounts; each had different criteria for being satisfied that the project was responsibly approaching its task. The Schools Council, representing a 'growth point' view of integrated studies, put pressure on the project to de-mythologise (even de-intellectualise) its models of integration and to work through the understandings of the trial school teachers, many of whom saw integration simply as combining traditional school subjects into a new content-based mesh. In the experience of the teachers 'integrated studies' was resource-based teaching around themes or topics taught by teams. On the other hand the academic audience of curriculum theorists were using and expecting accounts framed in terms of models, epistemological assertions and 'organising categories' of the curriculum. The two sides simply did not talk the same language.

The organisation of the project reflected these conflicts. The Director and Deputy Director were on the staff of the Keele Institute and were running courses in curriculum theory and practice. The L.E.A. 'coordinators' were middle men, cultural interpreters between the world of the teacher and the world of the academic.

Dissemination conferences tended to have multiple audiences (interested teachers, teacher educators, H.M.I.s etc.) and the view projected of the project was often an attempt to appease each segmont of the audience by a presentation calculated to appeal to its values, assumptions and basic beliefs. This manipulation of the personal imagery of project speakers was consistent right through to the details of the performance.

Returning to the G.Y.S.L. project and the accounts we have given of two project conferences we want to restate the nature of the 'communication problem' as this arises in dissemination. The point is this: curriculum dissemination is a social process in the course of which a group of curriculum developers have to negotiate successfully with many different groups who make different demands and hold different expectations. The social reality of the central project is a small group of people in a position that is temporary, marginal and precarious. Upon the success of these negotiations depends the survival of their work, and perhaps their personal career prospects. Many audiences must be satisfied, but we shall focus on two: the teachers and the academic community. The project must satisfy both these groups.

At Cambridge John Murrell said to the team in his talk, 'You had better not mention "needs" to a group of philosophers.' Dick Race (one of the teachers) said he wouldn't mention the word 'concepts' to his pupils. We want to ask, 'What don't you mention to geography teachers?' We suggest that, faced with the two audiences we have identified, projects employ two sets of responses to questions, implicit or explicit, about their view of the pupil, the discipline, and the teacher. What is the relationship between accepting, or condoning, a view of the pupil as severely handicapped, and the vision of the same pupil as an adult making complex personal and social judgements about the conduct of a modern, industrialised society?

Again at the Cambridge conference, Rex Gibson mentioned the tension between the project's remit and its subsequent development. Does this tension exist? If the aims of G.Y.S.L. are a common course, are they engaged in a smuggling operation? He also mentioned the threat to the teacher's identity, since identity is based on the knowledge the teacher possesses. Yet Rex Walford asked in the course of the conference: 'They know what geography is: why don't they make it explicit?' Surely because it is threatening. At the regional conference the notion of a 'new geography' was constantly played down: 'I don't know what people mean by it' was the answer one puzzled teacher got from a member of the team.

Rex Gibson also said that the project strategy embodied a consensus view of society. We would suggest that the project holds very much a conflict view of the society of education, seeing a conflict of values between the world of the practitioner and the world of Sockett, Lawton, Murrell, Gibson, Walford – and of MacDonald and Walker too – a world that is important because it is there that the project team negotiate their intellectual and professional identities.

'Who is the project for?' asked Gibson, 'and has the team got them right?' He had the pupils in mind, of course, but we would suggest that another answer is 'the teachers', and the second part of the question is still worth asking. 'Have they got *them* right?' 'Is there a relationship between classroom teaching and change in the higher reaches of academic geography and educational theory?' people keep asking. Of course there is, because the curriculum innovator has to negotiate with both groups. But the relationship is not a straightforward one – part of the gap between aspiration and implementation is the consequence of trade-off negotiations forced on one vulnerable group by two powerful groups characterised by mutually incompatible value systems. John Murrell said, speaking of how to motivate pupils, that it all boils down to compromise. You sum up the situation and do the best you can. Perhaps we have to ask of the Geography Project: Is theirs the right summing up, and the right compromise? Is the transmission, the 'message' to the teachers, strong enough to generate further development in the direction they hope for, or will it reinforce the curriculum they seek to change? What of the teacher who said of the project 'A gorilla could teach it'?

It is truer to say that projects speak with two emphases than to say that they speak with two voices. At the Cambridge conference the project team were constantly engaged in countering the 'counsels of perfection' of the academics by drawing attention to the practical difficulties of implementing radical change. At the training conference the project team members, in the small group sessions, worked hard to demonstrate to teachers how intellectually sophisticated tasks and ideas could be made acces-

72

sible to pupils by imaginative, well thought out approaches. The difference lies largely in what is defined as 'acceptable utilisation' of the project, and it is here that the difference is marked. A project aiming at mass implementation must define wide margins of acceptable use, at least initially, banking on continued contact with the user to provide opportunities to bridge the gap between its pedagogic aspirations and the user's pedagogic disposition and habits.

The project which attempts to gain the regard of both groups is likely to generate a double image. The critic's perception of the Geography Project featured the 'common course', the 'new geography', 'political education' and 'a change of teacher identity'. But, we believe, at least initially, many of the teachers looked to the project for a 'Newsom course' and a 'new-look geography'. This degree of latitude, which is sensitive to the teacher's self-esteem and to his need to retain his identity, is not easily reconcilable with the conditions of support laid down by the academic audience; for the latter, a substantial element of 'system threat' must be embodied in the innovation, and this element must not be compromised.

Stating the argument so starkly does violence to the reality. The 'double-image' often derives from qualities of the audience rather than ambiguity on the part of the project team, and audiences are more mixed than we have suggested. We emphasise too that the empirical evidence we have used is derived from one regional conference only, and that we have looked in detail at only the first few formal sessions. At this point the teachers had little or no experience of the project, and the stereotype we have set up may well break down with prolonged contact or (the team hopes) through the local groups. Moreover, curriculum negotiation as we have described it is not confined to this particular project, although it seems reasonable to suggest that the very extensive dissemination programme in which the Geography Project has engaged has by definition involved the team in more negotiating than less ambitious innovators have attempted. Again we emphasise that our account is limited to one part of one conference and looks at the *first impressions* we believe teachers had of the project, not at persistent judgements over a period of time. For the project team too the conference had a particular aim – to motivate teachers and spark off interest. From their point of view later project education could always be covered in the local groups.

All projects face the problem of developing curricula which match their own aspirations and meet with the approval of academic reference groups, and then of attempting to secure widespread adoption of their materials and approaches. Of course it is true that in this country classroom teachers are heavily involved in the development process and provide, along with evaluators, a great deal of feedback on the trial versions of materials. But it is the experience of most projects that such feedback is so lacking in uniformity, because of the large number of variables involved, that it provides, even when carefully scrutinised, little guidance for the developers, and only rarely a curb or setback to their ambitions. The Humanities Curriculum Project, for instance, produced packs of materials for discussion groups which contained many 'difficult' pieces. Despite extensive feedback procedures during the trial phase of the project, and despite a general conviction among most of the trial teachers that the reading level of the material was too high, very few individual items were described as too difficult by such a substantial majority of the teachers that there was a clear case for discarding them. The team was thus able to claim that the published materials had been successfully used by teachers. The experience of the Geography Project was similar.

Given the constraints that the curriculum innovators have to contend with, it is small wonder that they generate conflicting images, and often confusion. The Humanities Project claimed descent from the Newsom Report in its public pronouncements, seeking legitimation in social policy, but was in fact strongly opposed to almost everything in the Newsom Report except those excerpts it chose to quote. At the end of one five-day Humanities Project central training course, the project evaluator (one of the present writers) addressed the participants, and in the course of questioning mentioned the team's hostility to Newsom. The participants were non-plussed. 'But how can that be so?' one asked. 'We're all Newsom teachers here.'

To take another example, the Nuffield Science Projects: earlier in the book we quoted Becher's comments on the relative failure of innovations in the science field to make inroads into didactic teaching and passive pupil roles. It is clear that the implications of the new science curriculum for radical changes in the teacher's role were understood. 'If there is to be a "new look"

74

it will provoke a "new reaction". We must be prepared to approach our jobs with fresh eyes' (introduction to Nuffield 'O' Level Chemistry). It is equally clear that the implications were not to be followed through. 'This is a formidable problem and its solution depends on that personal creative art which is the essence of teaching.'

Scratch any project, and what emerges is a view of the relationships between knowledge, the teacher and the taught, a view of the organisational conditions required to support these relationships, and a view of the kind of institution in which such an organisation would be favoured (in all cases of significant innovation, these views are inconsistent with established practices). It would be possible to disseminate the new views, but not to negotiate them, and it is difficult to see how projects can improve their market performance without a corresponding increase in the degree to which they feel compelled to disguise the very conditions which would enable their work to survive and take root.

The Alternative Error? – H.C.P.: the dream merchants

In this chapter we have advanced a view of how national curriculum development projects negotiate their way into the schools by disguising, or more correctly by failing to emphasise, the full extent and nature of the changes which a faithful implementation of the innovation would bring about. Typically, we suggested, project teams go out of their way to avoid transmitting messages to teachers which explicitly or implicitly devalue established practice and threaten the teacher's self-esteem. This seems to be a peculiarly British response to the problem of securing curriculum change. Harry Broudy (1972) took American curriculum developers to task for failing to appreciate the dangers of basing their advocacy on an outright critique of the schools. 'Why the bright innovators are not bright enough to know that an offensive against a life work, against a cultural role, against personal significance will engender a defense is hard to understand.'

Projects like the Geography for the Young School Leaver Project have demonstrated how successful a dissemination strategy based on sensitivity in this area can be in attracting widespread teacher allegiance. The problem is of course how to reassure the practitioner without buttressing his previous practice. The Nuffield projects in secondary science took the view that the logic of the new materials themselves, combined with changes in the form of examination, were sufficient to bring about change of pedagogic approach in the classroom, and made unnecessary a direct challenge to the teacher's role and skills. The Geography Project's strategy for change, on the other hand, rests on the access to classrooms which they have created by the establishment of a national network of local teacher groups. In a sense, adoption and implementation *precede* development. For this strategy to work, it is essential that the network be serviced and maintained as a continuing 'temporary system', or become institutionalised at the local level. The project team are already negotiating with the Schools Council financial support that will enable central coordination to continue into 1977, but their efforts to 'transfer' their values and functions to local authority agents may prove to be a losing fight against time, vanishing resources, and resistance at the Authority level to the 'hand-me-down' nature of the transfer.

Not all projects in this country have chosen this particular strategy in trading with the teachers. The Humanities Curriculum Project, for instance, could be said to have offered the teacher a dream image of himself that was so far removed from his previous practice that it severed the very connections with it that are necessary to carry a critique. Let us see how far an analysis of H.C.P. will support this interpretation. We begin with a brief profile of the project from our SAFARI research study.

A profile of the Humanities Curriculum Project

Thumbnail social history of Humanities Curriculum Project

The team saw themselves as a 'research' group offering schools new knowledge and hypotheses about enquiry teaching, rather than prescribing a curriculum. 'We have nothing to recommend,' said Stenhouse. But teacher 'neutrality' was a provocative concept, and they were soon caught up in an inflationary spiral of rhetorical debate, at its most public when their collection of materials on Race was suppressed by the Schools Council in a blaze of publicity. Condemned by N.U.T. and N.A.S. spokesmen, cut adrift by the Council (though not by Nuffield),

76

and assailed variously from the Left ('bourgeois indoctrination'), from the Right ('dangerous revolution'), by academics ('ethnical relativism')', and by activists ('substituting social action with a parlour game'), the project was vigorously defended by an equally diverse range of allies, and acquired something of a 'cult' reputation while continuing to compete successfully in the market place.

Although H.C.P. was by no means an 'auteur project' (the team was large and unusually powerful), Stenhouse was a strong leader and remains an enigmatic figure: to admirers the most imaginative curriculum developer of them all ('a chess player in a world of draughts'), to detractors an over-intellectual entrepreneur. Welcomed with open jaws by the philosophers of education (he engaged in their discourse and invited curriculum analysis), disliked by the policy-makers (he wouldn't simplify, and cultivated paradox), he is, unlike most project directors, still active in the curriculum research field.

A one-sentence description
A five-year research, development, evaluation and dissemination programme concerned with the discussion by adolescent pupils of controversial social and moral issues.

The location and time scale
1967-70: Philippa Fawcett College, London.
1970-72: Centre for Applied Research in Education (CARE), University of East Anglia (initiative by Schools Council out of its growing concern for continuity and aftercare).

Cost
Approximately £250,000 (including evaluation)

Interpreting the remit
The team defined humanities as 'the study of important human issues', the aim of the project as 'to develop an understanding of human acts, of social situations, and of the problems of value which arise from them' and the curriculum problem as 'how is a teacher in a democracy to handle controversial value issues?'

Premises
The work of the project was based upon five major premises:

77

(1) that controversial issues should be handled in the class-room with adolescents;

(2) that the teacher accepts the need to submit his teaching in controversial areas to the criterion of *neutrality* at this stage of education, i.e. that he regards it as part of his responsibility not to promote his own view;

(3) that the mode of enquiry in controversial areas should have discussion, rather than instruction, as its core;

(4) that the discussion should protect divergence of view among participants, rather than attempt to achieve consensus;

(5) that the teacher as chairman of the discussion should have responsibility for quality and standards in learning.

Strategy

(a) *Materials:* nine themes were chosen as areas of enquiry for experimental development. The team produced multi-media collections of study materials and teacher guides in each theme area and in cooperation with the British Film Institute a film-hire service.

(b) *Pedagogy:* basically enquiry through classroom discussion, with the teacher, in the role of 'neutral chairman', attempting to promote reflective interpretation of 'evidence' drawn from the theme collections.

Dissemination

Aim: 'to establish by 1972 sufficient people throughout the country with understanding and energy enough to ensure that the experiment could be sustained, that new people could be effectively brought in, that experience could be shared and learned from and that standards could be effectively re-thought'.

Main Strategy: training through centrally-held courses, teams of people from L.E.A.s who then (at least theoretically) take responsibility locally for teacher training and support. Such courses, initiated in 1970, are still going on under the aegis of CARE, which maintains contact with a network of local contacts throughout the country.

The project's ideas and principles are difficult to grasp or have been poorly communicated, or both. *Exception:* the central courses which seem very effective and produce understanding and enthusiasm.

78

A guide to the observer of H.C.P.

(1) At the L.E.A. level

H.C.P. can be a risky enterprise for the teacher, both in career and political terms. Legitimation and informed external support are therefore important, especially when not provided by the school. Some L.E.A.s will back teachers who fear adverse community reaction, others firmly decline.

Training provision for new H.C.P. teachers essential

Hire of films for use in H.C.P. schools often depends on financial support from L.E.A.

(2) At the school level

Time allocation less important than viable group size, physical conditions (private and quiet) and access to materials (storage and retrieval are problems). Support of headmaster more important than that of colleagues. Danger of project being perceived as 'softsell' if confined to low status pupils and teachers. In schools with exam emphasis, some teachers say H.C.P. must be examined to gain commitment of staff and pupils. Others disagree, some hotly. Project Team stayed neutral on this issue.

(3) At the classroom level

Organisation: H.C.P. discussion difficult to realise with groups of more than 15 – mixed ability best, but no 'ad hoc' mixtures. Circular seating but semi-formal (i.e. with desks) best bet. Single sex groups disadvantaged with most themes. Experienced teachers more likely to succeed, even though more ingrained in previous practice.

Teacher role characteristics: does not express views, listens, summarises, controls interruptions, introduces new evidence, encourages pupils to concentrate on interpreting the materials, forestalls premature or social consensus on issues, tolerates silence, invites comment on his role performance.

Pupil role characteristics: addresses group rather than teacher, listens to views of others, refrains from personalised criticism, calls for new evidence, takes responsibility for maintaining the enquiry and for new initiatives.

Additional note

Adversaries of H.C.P. are critical of the difficulty level of the materials: advocates respond that the H.C.P. discussion process enables pupils to tackle successfully as a group materials they could not cope with as individuals. Adversaries claim that pupils must be able to understand the material *before* they can discuss it: advocates claim that understanding is the *product* not the *prerequisite* of discussion: 'You discuss because you do not understand.'

H.C.P. evaluation

Design
Combination of clinical, psychometric and sociometric studies. *Phase one* (1968-70): formative evaluation for central team, narrative chronicle of project history, case studies of trial schools *Phase two* (1970-73): measurement of pupil change, case studies of schools and L.E.A.s, surveys of adoption, studies of dissemination; extensive publication, mainly to participants, during this period.

Results
Case study: H.C.P. difficult to assimilate: schools much more authoritarian than they realise. H.C.P. creates dissonance at all levels of impact: persistence needed to achieve satisfaction and stability of process. Institutional context important but unpredictable. Individual pupil, teacher and school reactions range from dismal failure to spectacular success.
Measurement: test programme over-ambitious and seriously flawed in execution – nevertheless suggests that in the hands of trained teachers pupils gain in language skills and self-esteem.
Survey: adoption comparatively widespread – mainly by English and history teachers in mid-career. Family and War the favourite topics.

Overview of project impact
Considerable impact on professional debate about the role of the teacher and the responsibility of schools for moral education; some impact on curriculum and innovation theory; national impact on school practice largely unknown although commercially successful. The persistence of interest in H.C.P. may be a testimony to the importance of the problem or the remedy – or both.

Analysis

In what sense could this project be said to have offered a 'dream image' to teachers? John Berger (1972), analysing the effects of advertising, notes that the audience 'lives in the contradiction between what he is and what he would like to be . . . the gap between what the publicity actually offers and the future it promises corresponds with the gap between what the spectator-buyer feels himself to be and what he would like to be.' In a similar way the Humanities Project held out to the teacher a vision of what schools and teaching could become if they started from different premises. The promise was a future in which, through a process of redefinition of the relationship between teacher, taught, and knowledge, schools would be transformed into democratic institutions, teachers into research-based master craftsmen of a new professional tradition, and pupils (invariably called 'students' by H.C.P.) into reflective scholars. This future, conceivably, awaited those who accepted the invitation to recast themselves in a research role in the classroom, to follow the laid-down procedures, and to implement their 'findings' subsequently.

Stenhouse himself, in public transmissions of the project's work, likened H.C.P. discussions to university seminars and, on at least one occasion, to a romantic conception of medieval scholarship. It was a long way from the secondary modern school and 4Z, but many were seduced by the dream and tempted, by the powerful rhetoric and charisma of the project team, to undertake the journey. H.C.P. offered a genuine alternative to existing practice, a liberal and potentially liberating ideal. Many of the teachers who joined the 'crusade' found themselves imprisoned in a gap between the project's implicit model of the school and the realities of the institutional *milieux* in which they were located. Lots of them gave up H.C.P. A few, embittered by the experience, even gave up teaching as a career. But there were others who succeeded in breaking through to an innovative skill-based approach to humanities teaching which engendered a new sense of professionalism in the classroom and a high level of commitment to the project. The elitist undertones of the project (Stenhouse once expressed the view that H.C.P. might be suited only to an *élite* of schools, a view consistent with his basic suspicion of 'innovations' which have more than a 20 per cent success rate) were to find disturbing expression in the aftermath of transfer to local control. The following is a SAFARI report on H.C.P. training at the local level.

A key element in the dissemination of the Humanities Project was the notion of the central team as 'trainers of trainers'. The national training courses, still held twice a year by the project team, are intended both to enable people to practice 'neutral chairmanship' in their own schools and colleges, and also to provide them with the means for training others in their own schools and their own Authority. By all accounts the national courses have been highly successful.

The main intended outcome of the training courses is to give teachers access to a distinctive, novel, and highly disciplined pedagogy. An incidental effect has often been to create an in-group, with its own language, jokes, sensitivities and hostilities. Sometimes this group has been contained within a school, where existing social interactions and networks often mask or modify it, but when the network is established outside existing social relationships then the in-group phenomenon is emphasised. 'Packborough' L.E.A. is a large, urban Authority that for some years has supported H.C.P. Dissemination of the project is a responsibility of an inspector, himself occasionally a staff member on national courses, and well acquainted with the project and the project team. Through the efforts of the inspector, Packborough has established a network of experienced H.C.P. teachers and for some years has been running its own H.C.P. training courses. The central project team look on this development of autonomy as an achievement of some importance.

The point to note here is that the network established by the inspector, involving him and the team of experienced teachers who staff the conferences, exists where no strong network existed previously. Such a network, created in a social vacuum and based on the possession of complex skills, exhibits a strong mechanical solidarity. To watch the training course tutors in the bar before the course starts is reminiscent of other groups where identity is dependent on highly developed personal skills (it reminded me of similar meetings of mountaineering instructors).

What may seem from one point of view to be strong morale amongst the trainers may seem to a trainee to be an exclusive culture with rigorous, even exclusive, membership criteria. The cool professionalism which marks the trainers, and which they exercise with consummate skill in simulated discussions or on videotape, can have the effect of making membership of the in-group appear hard to achieve. But given a group of trainers which is itself a close social group, personal attributes as well as professional achievements can be seen as marking criteria of selection. This is emphasised in a situation like Packborough where the training team is long established and where many of its members have in fact been promoted to positions where their involvement in teaching the project has been reduced. Given a close group of experienced trainers established around the inspector the unintended effect of the training programme may be to show the project to large numbers of teachers, but to demonstrate its inaccessibility to all but a chosen few.

Compared with the Geography Project's 'open door' invitation, the Humanities Project acquired, without consciously seeking it, much more the image of an exclusive club, with election following a process of initiation designed to erase previous professional behaviour patterns and replace them with new ones. This effect of the project has a compelling irony when considered in the context of H.C.P.'s consistent intellectual attack upon authority-based knowledge.

For our present purpose it is enough to note that, instead of attempting to build links with existing teaching patterns, H.C.P. took the unusual step of spelling out quite explicitly a radical alternative to which established practice was largely irrelevant. Because its 'subject', values education, was as a formal category quite new, this was not seen by interested teachers as an attack on their existing professional identities, but as an opportunity to acquire an additional identity. Nor was it seen by them as an attack on their self-esteem, in the way that Broudy claims characterised the American innovators. Rather, the project's implicit assertion of feasibility clearly rested upon an assumption that teachers, provided with the right kind of support and encouragement, were capable of developing a high order of professional expertise. It was this assumption, in fact, that was rejected, sometimes contemptuously, by some of the American curriculum developers to whom the project was introduced in

1970. Speculatively, one could offer the interpretation that Stenhouse invited the teacher to create an alliance with him against the forces of institutional and attitudinal inertia in the school system. When the project fell foul of the 'authorities' (Schools Council and teachers' union leadership) over the 'Race Pack', the result was a significant spurt in sales and in teacher interest in H.C.P.

. In many ways the Humanities Curriculum Project and Geography for the Young School Leaver have comparable aspirations and overlapping curriculum interests, yet they chose demonstrably different responses to the problem of securing change in the schools. But H.C.P. had no subject allegiance, no set of subject-specific expectations to meet, no supervision from guardians of the discipline to contend with. It had neither the access to an established place in the school nor, on the other hand, the constraints that went with that access. Faced with the problem of carving out of a departmentalised curriculum a location for its work, it intuitively generated a prospect powerful enough to persuade teachers to depart from their secure territorial niches in order to explore its possibilities. It generated a single image, perhaps, but in many cases a significant and genuine gap between intent and practice. Many teachers are now engaged in attempting to bridge that gap through classroom action, but the dissonance that exists between the educational process as conceived by the project and that process as it is lived in the majority of schools may mean that some are imprisoned, like Berger's audience, in a gap that is 'filled with glamorous daydreams'.

Further reading
The Teachers' Guides to the three packs of materials produced by G.Y.S.L. Project form an essential background to this chapter (Schools Council 1973, 1974, 1975). The project's collection of papers, *Teachers Talking* (G.Y.S.L. 1974), provides accounts of the dissemination strategy.

Marten Shipman's account (1974) of the Keele Integrated Studies Project provides some comparative data of another project's attempts to resolve similar issues.

4 NUFFIELD SCIENCE — A CASE STUDY IN CURRICULUM EVOLUTION

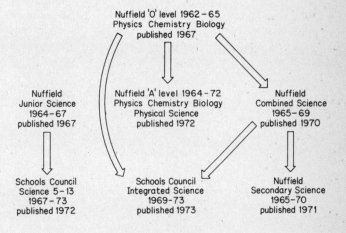

4.1 *Nuffield Science Teaching Project*

The age of curriculum dinosaurs?
The theme we want to take up in this chapter is that Nuffield Science is more accurately portrayed as one stage in a long tradition of curriculum innovation, than as a sudden curriculum cataclysm in the post-Sputnik era.

To portray Nuffield Science in this way demands a sense of history but this does not mean that we shall be presenting a purely historical account. Our focus is firmly set on the present, but just as biologists have altered their views about the nature of species since developing a sense of geological time, so our interpretations of curriculum change depend on our sense of history. In the nineteenth century many biologists thought in terms of an 'Age of the dinosaurs' as a clear period of time marked by cataclysmic changes in climate. It is only as biologists have learnt to appreciate the full extent of the time scale of evolution that the great Ages marked by geological discontinuity have been reinterpreted in terms of relatively minor changes. Even the 'Ice Age' may have meant an average temperature drop of only a few degrees.

If, in looking at Nuffield Science, we look back only to 1960, we are in danger of depicting the Nuffield Science movement as revolutionary or cataclysmic change; an epoch of curriculum dinosaurs perhaps preceded by a curriculum ice age.

But by extending our sense of history we can develop a different way of viewing the species. Instead of looking for dramatic cataclysm and revolutionary change, we can look for mutation and variation, for subtle shifts in climate which might cause readjustment in the balance of erosion and sedimentation, or in the creation and decay of landscape and habitat. In Schon's terms, we may be looking at a 'movement'.

To return directly to the subject of curriculum innovation, we can do no better than to quote a lecture given by Frank Musgrove to the First Standing Conference on Curriculum Studies at Exeter in 1973 (published in Musgrove 1975). Talking of the creation of new curricula as though they were mutations of existing practice, he said:

> We should understand the process which selects disreputable practices, makes them legitimate, and incorporates them into the stable core. How are they legitimised? Do they have to be sanctioned by HMIs, the School Council, particularly prestigious headmasters? Most so-called innovation is in fact the *diffusion* of legitimised and already routine and rather tired practices. Often it is thoroughly emasculated. Can we legitimise the disreputable most easily for diffusion in the low status areas of education? (Musgrove 1975)

Musgrove has the sense of history we have been referring to in relation to curriculum innovation. This is quite different from the view you often get from looking at the materials produced by curriculum development projects. Projects often present a view

86

of the curriculum area in which they work as one where the time is ripe for change. Only the inertia of traditional practice stands between the old and the new, between the irrational and the rational.

By labelling innovation as 'disreputable practice' ('mutation') Musgrove indicates that the change that underlies the spread of innovation is often a change in values. Just as in our biological analogy the spread of new species is dependent on changes in climate, so climate (in the sense of cultural climate) is significant in the diffusion of new curricula. He goes on to suggest a specific hypothesis we will be returning to in this chapter; that because new practice is disreputable, it can be diffused most easily in low status areas of education.

A brief history of Nuffield Science

A chronology 1900-62

1900 Association of Public School Science Masters (A.P.S.S.M.) formed: the first professional association of science teachers.

1904 *Regulations for Secondary Schools* issued under the 1902 Education Act establish science in the secondary school curriculum.

1916 A.P.S.S.M. publish *Science for All*, a plea for a general approach to the teaching of science for all (public school) boys.

1918 Thomson Report published.

1919 A.P.S.S.M. includes non-public school masters and is reconstituted as the Science Masters' Association (S.M.A.).

1920 Science Masters' Association publish *Science for All – a Plea for General Science*.

1946 Barlow Report recommends doubling the output of scientists from higher education.

1957 S.M.A. publish provisional policy statement: 14,000 copies sold.

1960 Ministry of Education publish Pamphlet 38, *Science in Secondary Schools*.

1961 S.M.A./A.W.S.T. publish *Science and Education: A Policy Statement*, proposing curriculum development in separate

sciences at 'O' level.
1962 Nuffield Science Teaching Projects announced; S.M.A./A.W.S.T. becomes Association for Science Education (A.S.E.).

In 1961 the Minister of Education (David Eccles) made a brief statement in the House of Commons. He announced that the Nuffield Foundation had agreed to finance the development of new courses in school science. Initially these courses were to be of 'O' level standard in physics, chemistry and biology, and they were to be developed mainly by teachers seconded from schools.

Behind the Minister's brief statement lies a long, complex, and still largely untold story. The immediate context was a link between the Nuffield Foundation and the science teachers' professional association (now the A.S.E. – the Association for Science Education, but existing since 1901 under a variety of titles, particularly as the S.M.A. – the Science Masters' Association).

Reduced to its elements the story was that the Nuffield Foundation, drawing its revenue from the Morris car empire (now British Leyland), was accumulating money faster than they were spending it. Not only was car production in a phase of peak prosperity, but the areas of research traditionally funded by the Foundation (particularly medicine) were increasingly being taken over by government agencies. The Foundation had a policy of supporting research in areas not financed by the government and so were looking for new areas of investment. One area that interested them particularly was technical and technological education at college level, but although some grants were given no major projects were funded (a full account is given in Clark 1972).

While the Nuffield Foundation were looking for projects to fund, the A.S.E. was looking for money. Always a strong professional association, it had, during the fifties, begun to press hard for curriculum reform, and in 1961 had published a *Policy Statement*. It was this policy statement that formed the basis of the proposal to Nuffield and to the establishment of the Nuffield Science Teaching Project.

Looking back at the policy statement it seems that the A.S.E. (then the Science Masters' Association and the Association of Women Science Teachers) was strongly influenced by the climate created by the C. P. Snow-Leavis controversy, and the theme of the 'Two Cultures' (Snow had given his famous lecture in 1959). The policy statement makes a strong claim for science as culture:

> Science should be recognised – and taught – as a major human activity which explores the realm of human experience, maps it methodically but also imaginatively, and by disciplined speculation, creates a coherent system of knowledge. As a human quest for Truth – and it is much more subjectively human than is often realised – science is concerned with basic values and is, indeed, an active humanity.
>
> (Science Masters' Association 1961, p.5)

This bid for science as culture was aimed particularly at the grammar school curriculum. The statement's central recommendation was that 'science should be a 'core' subject in grammar schools in the same way as, for example, English and mathematics are at present and as classics used to be.' (ibid.).

Musgrove's hypothesis, that innovation spreads more easily in low status areas of the curriculum, begins to look more complex than it did at first sight. Nuffield Science was initially wholly concerned with the 'O' level grammar school courses. While these might be thought of as low status relative to the public schools, they still concerned only a relatively narrow élite selection of schools, teachers and pupils. And could science itself really be considered as a low status area of the curriculum relative to English and mathematics?

We asked Tony Mansell, a chemist who had worked on the Nuffield 'A' level project and who has an active interest in the history of science teaching, whether or not the intense activity of Nuffield Science could be seen in any way as a bid for status against other curriculum areas. He agreed that fifty years ago science teachers had felt themselves to be undervalued:

> The late Victorian attitude in the public schools was that science and modern subjects were not really the sort of subjects for gentlemen . . . and in the 1920s there were still presidential addresses [to the S.M.A.] which contained statements like, 'the science master has only recently emerged from being on the same level as the French master, and lower than that

you cannot go'. I think the decay of the classics had started much earlier [than Nuffield], in Edwardian times they were under severe attack and certainly the First World War justified science as part of the curriculum because it was quite obvious what happened if you didn't have it. The situation was really acute – we got all our dyes for uniforms from Germany; in spite of the fact that it was an Englishman who had invented the dyes, it was the Germans who made them all. Fuses, all the optical equipment, came from Germany, not from Britain. The Germans had better quality steel, and all this was because the Germans had a better supply of scientific manpower. (SAFARI interview)

Science was established as a part of the school curriculum by the first world war. What followed was less a debate about whether or not it should be taught than a debate about *how* it should be taught. On the one hand, it was included in the curriculum because of its utility, and because of its significance for technology. On the other hand, many of those who taught it did so as much out of respect for its cultural significance as for its utility, a feeling strongly expressed in the A.S.E.'s 1961 policy statement.

Nuffield Science as symptom
Our central theme in this chapter is that Nuffield Science can be seen as one stage in a continuing debate in which the tension lies between a view of science as a source of technical knowledge, and a view of science as a contribution to culture. Expressed more conventionally the debate is between science as information and techniques to be learnt, and science as knowledge to be gained by the extension of imagination and understanding.

Science teaching became part of the school curriculum during the nineteenth century. The debate between the two views of science we are following grew out of the different arguments used to establish science in the schools at that time. Before we attempt to follow this debate more closely we should remember just how small was the scale of science teaching at that time. In their *Social History of Education in England* (1973), John Lawson and Harold Silver write: 'The Devonshire Commission reported in 1875 on the teaching of science in public and endowed schools ... "The better endowed schools had been circulated and of the

90

128 who replied, science was stated to be taught in 63. Only 13 had a laboratory and 18 any apparatus." ' They go on to point out that it was only in 1904, in a regulation issued under the 1902 Education Act, that schools were required to teach science. Yet even as late as 1918, when following the clear superiority of German technical education revealed by the first world war the Thomson Report set out to describe the state of science teaching in schools, they found that in a considerable number of schools science took up as little as four three-quarter hour periods a week and sometimes less. Not only was the quantity of science teaching rather small, but what actually went on in those few lessons was not necessarily anything we would recognise today as part of an independent discipline. Summarising his studies of nineteenth century pioneers in science teaching, David Layton writes:

> There is no escaping the conclusion that, by the mid-nineteenth century, science had made little progress in establishing itself as a basic element in general education. Where scientific knowledge did appear in the curriculum it frequently served religious or moral ends . . . or was introduced because of its utility. Elsewhere it was justified . . . in terms of the exercise of postulated faculties of mind such as those of 'observation' or 'classification'. There was little recognition of science as a distinct mode of understanding. (Layton 1973)

To underline the point, the extract David Layton gives from a demonstration lesson in 'scriptural natural history' dating from the 1840s dramatically illustrates how science was reinterpreted into the conventional curriculum:

Teacher: Yes, the heat melts it; and then what becomes of all the earthy substances which are mixed with the silver? (a pause) They rise to the top and the silver remains at the bottom. And what do you think the man who is refining the silver does then to get rid of the impurities? I think some of you have seen your mothers do something of the same kind.

Children: Skim it.

Teacher: Yes, the man skims off what is at the top. Now, what is it that separates the impure substances

	from the silver?
Children:	The heat of the fire.
Teacher:	Tell me the two things about which the refiner is careful.
Children:	He is careful not to take the silver out of the fire till it is pure; and he is careful not to keep it there when it is pure.
Teacher:	And how does he know?
Children:	When it is pure it reflects his image.
Teacher:	Now, dear children, I have given you this lesson on refining silver, to lead you to understand what Jesus Christ does for us. Listen to this passage of Scripture. Speaking of the Lord Jesus Christ, it says, 'He shall sit as a refiner and purifier of silver, and he shall purify his people, and purge them as gold and silver, that they may offer to the Lord an offering in righteousness.'
	(These words read by the teacher twice.) Who is spoken of here?
Children:	Christ.
Teacher:	Who shall sit?
Children:	Christ.
Teacher:	As what shall he sit?
Several voices:	As a refiner.

The science that did establish itself in the curriculum was content-laden, and the teaching was mainly by rote learning from the textbook. The only body awarding qualifications was the Department of Science and Art, and its examinations were based mainly on recall; there was little requirement for practical work.

This is not to say that the situation was not under scrutiny. The Devonshire Report, published in the 1870s, noted the slowness with which schools were taking up science, but commented:

We are not prepared to assert that the mere communication to the mind of the pupil of the facts of science would contribute very materially to the training of his intellectual powers, although it may supply him with much valuable information, and may render him the still more important service of awakening his desire for further knowledge. But the true teaching of science consists, not merely in imparting the facts of science, but in habituating the pupil to observe for himself, to reason for himself on what he observes, and to check the conclusions at which he arrives by further observation or experiment. (McLure 1965)

The debate between those who saw science as content to learn, and those who saw it as knowledge to be understood, was beginning to form. The key figure who brought it to life was Henry Armstrong. A professor of chemistry, trained in Germany, Armstrong became concerned that the students he taught (particularly the medical students he taught at St Bartholomew's Hospital) were lacking in any understanding of scientific method. He became concerned about the kind of science that was being taught in schools and set out to shift the emphasis away from content and into method.

Although the debate was engaged in by others, it was Armstrong who took action. With the philosophy of 'heurism', which he described as using 'methods of teaching which involve our placing students as far as possible in the attitude of the discoverer' (Armstrong, quoted in Nuffield Chemistry 1967), he attacked the existing system at several points. His students went out into schools and into the inspectorate and attempted to practise what he preached. He became a governor of Christ's Hospital and worked to establish it as a living demonstration of his philosophy. (Which to some extent it remains. One of the Nuffield 'O' level chemistry project team was seconded from the school.)

Although the ideas promulgated by Armstrong were not entirely original (see, for example, Brock 1971), it was Armstrong who through his actions focused the debate: 'He provided syllabuses, provided a curriculum, he switched the . . . arguments about *why* science should be taught, to *how* it should be taught; from arguments about the merit of individual science to the value of scientific method *per se*' (Brock 1971).

Even in the condensed and simplified version of the story we have told here, there are two dimensions which relate back to the issues we raised in chapter 1, where we looked at the theories of dissemination and implementation. When we trace the history of the British science curriculum over the last hundred years or so we can see two major processes at work. One is the spread of the science curriculum itself as a 'new invention', becoming established on a rapidly increasing scale in an education system that itself has been expanding and changing. At this level the problem looks very like the problems examined by the theorists of innovation like Shoemaker and Schon. Essentially the key criteria are criteria of uptake and persistence, and adoption can almost be assessed by the study of a collection of timetables.

The other question we have looked at is one that is less visible to normal bureaucratic procedures. It is one thing for science to become established as part of the curriculum, but what kind of science? Questions of content and approach are elusive but significant.

What we have tried to emphasise in this chapter is that such questions are endemic; they do not simply follow as a second phase to adoption. Science cannot be established as a part of the curriculum without the question 'What kind of science?' being raised. Any curriculum reform movement is, in consequence, likely to have its antecedents.

Postscript to the history of the heuristic movement

As we contemplate the current scene and look at the way Nuffield Science has been absorbed by the educational system we cannot repress some curiosity at the fate of the heuristic movement. Is there a straight line of contact between Armstrong and Nuffield, or did heurism die out? The answer seems to be that although the tradition was kept alive in some places, heurism died out as a movement with the publication of the Thomson Report in 1918.

The Thomson Committee saw part of the failure of British technical achievement in the first world war as stemming from the fact that:

In many schools more time is spent in laboratory work than the results obtained can justify. We do not underestimate the importance of such work; on the contrary we regard it as an essential part of science teaching. But sometimes the performance of laboratory exercises has been considered too much an end in itself – such an exercise loses the educational value of a real experiment when it becomes a piece of drill.

Armstrong had advocated practical work as an alternative to rote learning and content-laden courses and had campaigned to get more laboratory space and equipment into schools. Yet within twenty years the innovation had become orthodoxy, so that where Armstrong had aspired to 'put the beginner absolutely in the position of an original discoverer', Thomson found 'drill'.

Parallels with the present

In terms of the overall debate between discovery learning and didactic teaching methods there are distinct parallels between the nineteenth-century debate and the Nuffield Science movement. On the other hand there are also distinct differences. The heuristic movement, like the curriculum reform movement in the U.S.A., had largely been initiated by professional scientists (Armstrong, Frankland, Spencer, Huxley and other members of the 'X' Club – Brock 1971), whereas the S.M.A.'s pressure for reform in the fifties and sixties came almost entirely from teachers.

It is interesting that a number of the teachers active in the S.M.A. were people who had come into teaching during the thirties. Many were not only highly qualified, but were people of considerable ability who came into teaching at a time when jobs in industry or research were hard to find. Several of the key figures were from working class or lower middle class backgrounds, and saw science as a basically class-free endeavour and their own education as critically important in their lives. Consequently they often developed strong commitments both to science and to education.

Ernest Coulson (who has been a key figure in the Nuffield chemistry projects) has written an autobiographical account of Nuffield Science which illustrates the point. He left school in 1925 unqualified in chemistry and, as he put it, 'clearly I was not university material so I had to find a job'. Through a Sunday School teacher he applied for a job as a laboratory attendant at Woolwich Arsenal, and there 'I caught my enthusiasm for chemistry . . . from practising chemists enjoying what they did and eager to add to their knowledge'. From this chance sparking of interest he went on to a part-time degree course at Woolwich Polytechnic, then to Imperial College and later to do research at

Cambridge before he took a teaching post at Braintree Grammar School, where he was to remain for more than thirty years before joining the 'O' level chemistry project team in 1964. But his entry to teaching was again largely chance: he shared the opinion of his fellow chemists that 'if all else failed one could always teach – this was thought to be within the capabilities of us all!' (Coulson, 1972).

Another major distinctive feature of Nuffield Science when compared to the heuristic movement was its strong sense of curriculum design. Materials were produced and then given field trials before publication. As the projects proceeded it became clear that field testing was important not simply as a feature of the design process, but as an element of what came to be called diffusion (and later still, 'dissemination'). The trial schools formed both a reservoir of experience and a springboard for extending use of the project more widely.

Yet it would be a mistake to assume that the early Nuffield projects aspired to mass sales and widespread change. Certainly Frank Halliwell, organiser of the 'O' level chemistry project, saw the injection and development of new ideas as more significant than 'selling' the project. He and his team used the project to work out a philosophy strongly based on their teaching experience, which they used to reorientate chemistry teaching. 'We stopped looking at the subject and deciding *how* it should be taught, and instead we looked first at the child and at how he thinks and learns, and only then did we look at the subject . . .' (SAFARI interview 1973). It is important to stress that this shift away from the primacy of the structure of the subject to the ways of thinking of the pupil was not tied to particular theories in the philosophy of science or in psychology. The stance of the project was one which emerged from contemplation of experience of teaching over a number of years rather than as a response to particular theories.

This emphasis on the particular situation raises again the issue of parallel invention or spread from single centres, for Nuffield Science, which seems in many ways a home-grown product grounded in the particular history of British science and British education, nevertheless has strong parallels with the American science curriculum reform movement. Both, more or less independently, arrived at versions of an objectives model and worked to a design that formed a prototype for Havelock's R, D

96

and D model. It is clear that there was contact between curriculum developers in Britain and America, but their own view of the situation was one in which the excitement of what they were doing seemed more important than the international exchange of theory.

Having thought through their philosophy, the team – Nuffield 'O' level chemistry for example – found themselves with rather radical ideas. It took them six months to produce a syllabus – 'and when we did produce a syllabus, it didn't have the name of a single chemical in it!' (Halliwell, in SAFARI interview 1973). In all the 'O' level projects the teams felt themselves close to immediate teaching situations and there was little attempt to concede to mainstream opinion amongst science teachers. Each project had fairly clear ideas about what was needed. The chemists worked their way intuitively towards something closely resembling Bloom's taxonomy of objectives and talked about 'Education through chemistry'. The physicists stressed the phrase 'science for understanding'. The biologists struggled to bring experimental methods into a field dominated by description. In each subject what was attempted was seen by teachers as ambitious and controversial.

Although they were ambitious, another feature of the early projects was their accurate appraisal of practical difficulties, not only in the sense of spending a great deal of time working on new apparatus and equipment, but also in realising the difficulties created by examination boards. Within a few weeks of starting work, the chemistry team had secured the opportunity of developing an alternative 'O' level exam with the London Board and one of the team (John Mathews) subsequently spent most of his time developing new forms of exam and new kinds of question. (Interestingly, one of the first moves the project made was to drop the practical exam.) The other 'O' level projects soon acquired similar conditions from other boards. The rationale for this was to protect those children involved in the experimental trials of materials, but once the alternative examinations were established they represented rather more than procedural protection, they became an aspect of the process of change.

Nuffield Science as a catalyst
We have suggested that Nuffield Science can be seen as

belonging to a tradition of innovation in science teaching which has its origins in the nineteenth century. Though the projects had distinctive novel features, especially in their organisation and design, the ideas they were seen to represent were not fundamentally new. Nevertheless, Nuffield Science can be seen as a catalyst for further change, some of which must have been unanticipated at the time of development.

Perhaps most significant was the fact that the Nuffield projects set the scene for the curriculum reform movement. It is interesting to speculate whether the Schools Council would have been set up, or would have operated in quite the way it did, if the Nuffield projects had not first blazed the trail.

Within science teaching Nuffield projects have always appeared to steer a delicate line between radical change and conservatism, but the debate has had its effects, for there can be no doubt that moves into integrated science (S.C.I.S.P.) and toward science for the non-examination pupil (secondary science) have been focused by the earlier Nuffield projects which were significant in forming opinion as well as in changing the curriculum of schools.

Concluding comments

The Nuffield Science Teaching Project initiated the curriculum reform movement in this country, and because it was first in the field, development naturally played a much greater part than dissemination. As Frank Halliwell, organiser of the 'O'. level chemistry project, commented in an interview: 'At the time we weren't really interested in how many schools, or how many teachers 'did' the project. We were asked to produce a course based on our philosophy. And this is it.' (SAFARI interview, 1973).

Similar conditions had met the early projects in the U.S.A. which had 'considered their task completed when they had produced materials that, in their judgement, met the initial or emergent aims of the project' (Grobman 1970, p. 148). Thus CHEM Study 'arranged for private publication of materials and distributed the book itself . . . sending a sample copy to every high school chemistry teacher in the United States, with the assumption that the materials would sell themselves without the usual promotional campaign, and without salesmen visiting the schools' (Grobman 1970, p. 153).

However, the idea of diffusion by merit had disadvantages we pointed out earlier. It may have been effective in getting projects into fifty per cent of schools within five years but there often appeared to be considerable distortion of the message.

> Thus one comes across cases where materials (for example those of Nuffield 'O' level physics) essentially devised to exploit discovery methods are in fact being used in traditionally didactic ways; and others where materials (for instance those for audiovisual language courses) designed to encourage active pupil participation, are being employed largely for passive rote learning. It turns out that not even the most carefully designed materials are 'user-proof' in the sense that they clearly carry their own implications and are impervious to individual differences in the skills and attitudes of the teachers who use them. (Becher 1971)

The notion of 'teacher-proof packages' had certainly been considered by the Nuffield Science Teaching Project. John Lewis was said to have returned from a visit to the U.S.S.R. full of enthusiasm for teacher-proof packages and reputedly saying, 'In Russia they have very many bad science teachers but very few bad science lessons'. In general, however, teacher-proof packages had been rejected on the grounds of their violation of teaching method, which the developers saw as an 'art' protected by teacher autonomy.

Frank Halliwell's stance as critic and philosopher, unconcerned with the success of the product, can perhaps now be seen as the luxury of being first in the field. Certainly it would have been a difficult stance for G.Y.S.L. to have taken, given the climate of the late sixties. Even Lawrence Stenhouse had to work hard to defend a similar position for the Humanities Curriculum Project. (He used to open *dissemination* conferences by beginning, 'We have nothing to recommend . . .')

Before we leave Nuffield Science we need to make some comments on Havelock's R, D and D model. The 'Nuffield model', as it has sometimes been called, is often equated with the R, D and D model, and it does share some of its characteristics: an emphasis on materials production, on their field trial and the use of an objectives model to link materials and actions. There are, however, significant ways in which the story of the Nuffield Science Teaching Project departs from the pure form of the model.

First, the early projects (and it is rather less true of Junior Science, Secondary Science and Schools Council Integrated Science) already had a strong social interaction network (an insemination network) built into the design before funding. The long run-up to the projects through S.M.A. committees, meetings and conferences created the basis which made much of the later work possible. (For example, recruitment of trial schools and initial diffusion of project materials.) In the event, the projects exemplified a much less pure form of the R, D and D model than is commonly supposed. In fact, we can pursue the point even further and question the extent to which the projects can be identified with Schon's central-periphery model, for in some sense the invention rested with the users. Certainly the projects are a long way from Ernest House's notion of the R, D and D model, which conjures up images of curricula being written in Washington by non-teachers and imposed on unwilling school systems and teachers.

Further reading

The single most significant study in the area covered by this chapter is Mary Waring's Ph.D. thesis (1975), which examines the origins of Nuffield Science and the events that led to the setting up of the projects, and goes on to look in some detail at the development process in the 'O' level biology and chemistry projects.

Curiously the longer-term history has been studied more carefully than recent events and the literature offers more options. Nevertheless the whole field of the history of science education is surprisingly thin. Lawson and Silver (1973) provide the outlines of the story and David Layton's account (1973) is very interesting on the nineteenth century pioneers of school science teaching, especially in the illustrative material it includes. Brock's essay (1971) takes up the story from the point at which Layton leaves it and traces some of the social and political networks behind the heuristic movement at the end of the nineteenth century.

For those with the time to look them up, back numbers of the *School Science Review* provide an interesting source of material, especially in the published speeches given by S.M.A. presidents and the obituaries of leading figures in science education (for example Armstrong's obituary in the 1936 volume).

5 PROJECT TECHNOLOGY – A CASE STUDY IN CURRICULUM INSEMINATION

In chapter 3 we looked in some detail at the dissemination of the Geography for the Young School Leaver project. In this chapter we want to look at another Schools Council project, located in a different subject area and working with quite a different strategy for planning educational reform.

The Geography for the Young School Leaver Project team invested much of its effort in the development of materials, their trial use in schools and their dissemination to schools. Broadly speaking the aim was to produce materials that would receive wide circulation but which would also serve to carry the philosophy of the project team. Following the outline of the R, D and D model, the assumption behind the large-scale dissemination plan was that adoption would precede implementation.

As we have seen in the last chapter, the messages carried by G.Y.S.L. include the attempt to change the kind of geography taught in school away from descriptive accounts demanding factual recall to something closer to scientific geography; the attempt to shift content from rural to urban themes; the attempt to introduce a form of the objectives model into geography teaching; and the attempt to extend the preserve of geography teaching to include the discussion of value areas. A close look at the packs produced by the team reveals how this collection of attempts to change practice provides a structure around which the materials are organised and formulated. The attempt to change the curriculum by publication of materials which have been written to embody particular ideas and values is a common one. 'Materials production' forms a basic activity for most Schools Council and Nuffield curriculum projects. G.Y.S.L. exemplifies a common theme.

In this chapter we want to look at another project, the Schools Council project, Project Technology. Project Technology took a quite different approach to the problem of dissemination. Geoffrey Harrison, the project director, resisted the idea (that had become virtually dogma in the curriculum development field) that materials production was the central activity in curriculum development. The project did produce materials, but equally: 'The efforts of the central team concentrated on bringing together suggestions for new activities in technological education and on building up a network of co-operating teachers who could participate in training programmes in local development work and in spreading the gospel to colleagues in their own areas' (Becher 1971, p. 6). Becher identifies this strategy with Havelock's social interaction model and predicts that in practice there will be two weaknesses inherent in it. One he sees in its assumption that 'all teachers share sufficient of the characteristics of those who are most energetic and creative . . .'; the other that once the central team disbands then social networks will fragment and disperse.

Harrison rejected the means rather than the ends of the R, D and D model. ('Perhaps not consciously,' he recalls, 'I was a complete tiro with respect to the profession of curriculum development, and the models you refer to even now leave me cold!') Nevertheless he felt the central problem was 'that before anything could be done the important thing was to bring about a change of attitude to technology' (SAFARI interview 1974). 'A change of attitude', he felt, was better achieved through development of support agencies than through the investment of resources in the production and testing of exemplary materials which could only have been used with a narrow range of pupils. In this sense the project exemplifies not only Havelock's 'social interaction' strategy but also, in its attempts to create support for 'continually changing teaching', Schon's 'self-transforming model'. It provides us with a study in curriculum 'insemination', an attempt to create the kind of context and structure which supported innovation in science.

Information on Project Technology

Sponsor: Schools Council
Location: Loughborough College of Education

Duration: 1966 (pilot year)
1967-70 (main project)
1970-72 (extension)

Grant: £270,000

Main publications:

(a) Fifteen teachers' handbooks published by Heinemann (sample titles: *Simple Bridge Structures, Simple Fluid Flow, Industrial Archaeology*)

(b) Technology briefs: work card style presentation of suggestions for projects (Heinemann)

(c) Courses in electronics and control technology (C.S.E. level) and engineering science ('A' level)

(d) *Bulletin:* a journal for schools

(e) SATIS: an abstract service for teachers

People:

Geoffrey Harrison (project director)

Edward Semper (author of the original proposal)

Derek Morrell, Robert Morris and John Banks (Schools Council staff)

Terry Page (Institute of Mechanical Engineers)

Sir Peter Venables, D. R. O. Thomas and Basil de Ferranti (captains of industry)

Harold Wilson (Prime Minister)

Prince Philip (Duke of Edinburgh)

Thumbnail history of the project

Part one

The project grew from different roots and gained support from several social networks. Perhaps most significant was the Association of Heads of Secondary Technical Schools, the group who, under the leadership of Edward Semper, made the approach to the Schools Council which led to the establishment and funding of the project.

Semper was head of a technical grammar school in Doncaster, and shared with other members of the Association a commitment to the notion embodied in the Crowther Report as the 'Alternative Road'. This proposed an alternative but equal approach to academic education on the assumption that 'some boys learn best by deducing from applications rather than reasoning from principles'. The A.H.S.T.S. were concerned

104

that, following the implementation of the 1944 Education Act, very few Authorities were in fact establishing a fully tripartite system in which grammar, technical and modern schools offered a full range of opportunities to the community. They saw the traditions of technical education, and the promise of the 'Alternative Road', shrinking in the face of what was becoming nationally a predominantly bipartite system of secondary schooling.

This background is important to stress, because although the activity of A.H.S.T.S. was eventually expressed in terms of a proposal to develop 'technology' in schools, early papers indicate a much wider educational concern.

In 1963 Semper secured secondment from his L.E.A. to Sheffield University where he formed a Development Committee under the chairmanship of Boris Ford (then Professor of Education at Sheffield University) and including academics, industrialists and H.M.I.s. The minutes of the early meetings of this group reveal that discussions were around the theme of a possible 'enquiry . . . into the factors affecting the intellectual curiosity of adolescents and the use of personal investigation as a means of learning'. Key elements in the discussion were the notions of 'creative problem solving' (as opposed to 'theory' and 'abstract ideas') and 'inventive thinking'.

The emerging proposal was not just for the inclusion of a new element in the curriculum – 'technology' – but engaged long-standing ideas about education which embodied their own theories of learning. Although these ideas later became submerged in Project Technology, they remained a strong underlying theme. The phrase 'creative problem solving' continually recurs in Project Technology, and its importance to the project is marked amongst other things by appearances of Edward de Bono at project-sponsored conferences.

Two other events need to be noted in the run-up to Project Technology. One was the publication, in 1965, of a report by G. T. Page called *Engineering Among the Schools*. Page was information officer for the Institution of Mechanical Engineers. The institution had shown some concern about the quality of recruitment to engineering (a research study by Hutchings, published in 1963 and given some publicity at the time, had shown that the more able sixth formers were tending to opt away from engineering and applied science). The Page Report attempted to survey 'good practice' in the schools in the field of applied science and engineering, and in itself became a contributory factor in the press for the development of school technology.

Second, D. I. R. Porter, a staff inspector in H.M.I., was commissioned by the Schools Council to write Curriculum Bulletin No 2, 'A School Approach to Technology'. Writing at the same time as Page, Porter made a strong case for increasing the applied science element in the secondary school curriculum.

Even from this brief survey we can see that before a proposal was formally made to the Schools Council several organisations were involved in preliminary negotiations – the Association of Heads of Technical Schools, Sheffield University, H.M.I., and the Institution of Mechanical Engineers. Semper also made a further set of contacts amongst industrialists. He was, remember, working before the creation of Schools Council when the only likely source of funding was the Nuffield Foundation. Nuffield, however, was fully occupied with the Nuffield Science projects and so Semper started making contacts in industry. He contacted the Committee of Principals of Colleges of Advanced Technology, the Education Committee of the Federation of British Industry (now the C.B.I.) and the British Employers' Federation. (It was on a suggestion of Sir Peter Venables that Semper contacted Boris Ford of Sheffield University and later obtained secondment as 'part-time lecturer at the institute for one term'.)

He succeeded in gaining some patronage from D.R.O. Thomas of the British Steel Corporation, who as a representative of the F.B.I. began raising funds through holding dinner parties for fellow industrialists. All these promises of funding were conditional on matched funding from a government or educational source, but Semper found it difficult to get a response through the usual channels, so in 1964, as Harold Wilson rode to power on a campaign highly charged by the rhetoric of a coming 'white hot age of technology', Semper wrote directly to the new Prime Minister. He was invited to meet Derek Morrell and Robert Morris, Joint Secretaries of the newly-formed Schools Council, to discuss his proposal.

Semper's meeting with the new Schools Council secretariat left him and his committee with a choice: if they wanted to remain independent and to use the industrial money promised them then they could expect a grant of about £10,000 from the

Schools Council. If they were to hand the project over to the Council then the Council could develop it as a full project and fund it about £100,000. Semper and his committee decided to hand over control to the Schools Council.

In May 1965 the Schools Council held a conference at Belgrave Square. Nominally, the aim was to discuss current developments in the field of school technology. But a strong hidden agenda was that this was a chance for the Schools Council staff to look at potential project directors. Amongst those who attended were Semper, Somerhoff from Sevenoaks School, Don Porter, John Maddox, Terry Page, and the newly-appointed head of the Design Department at Loughborough College of Education, Geoffrey Harrison. Harrison had been a practising civil engineer and had taught at Dartmouth Naval College and Dauntsey's School. At Dauntsey's School he had built up the engineering department with a strong emphasis on individual project work. Don Porter had visited the school whilst writing Curriculum Bulletin No 2 and had been impressed by what he had seen. At the Belgrave Square conference he also impressed the Schools Council staff, who found him a man of ideas, interested in social policy and not just in making sixth form science more technologically orientated. The group also felt that he had the multiple skills of the project director – the skills of the salesman, the diplomat and the negotiator. It was difficult for the Schools Council to negotiate with Loughborough for Harrison's release to work on the project, but eventually these problems were overcome and Harrison was appointed project director. It is worth noting that Harrison was an outsider to the project's pre-history, and that he only got to hear Semper's story some time later, and then informally. Such is the nature of temporary institutions.

Part two
We have looked so far at the background to the project, at the people and events involved before the project existed as such. This background is important because it contains the seeds of what later turned out to be significant issues. Such seeds include the role of the project in keeping alive the 'creative problem solving' tradition – a tradition of education stemming back at least to the Crowther Report; the interest and involvement of the professional institutions, especially those concerned about fal-

ling standards of recruitment to the profession; the canvassing of industrial support at high management levels and the 'capturing' of the experience of a small number of schools actively developing technology courses (Sevenoaks, Gateway School in Leicester, Dauntsey's School, Danum Grammar School). It was the fitting together of these overlapping but separated interest groups that made Project Technology viable, but once incorporated each interest group then became, in a sense, a lobby within the project's audience. Even before the project began it already had traditions and expectations written into an invisible charter. For a project that was to operate within the 'social network' model, it is interesting to see how many networks were already forged by the conception of the project, before the development phase began.

Developing a design

It was in the context of the situation we have sketched that Project Technology took the decision to give as much of its attention to developing agencies of support for teachers as to producing materials. Geoffrey Harrison took the broad view that Project Technology should not simply be concerned with developing technology as a novel item in the school curriculum, but that it should address the more general problem of changing the way in which the whole curriculum was viewed. This breadth of vision was one of the things that had impressed Morrell, Morris, Banks and others at the Schools Council.

In part the nature of the curriculum determined the nature of the design. Whereas the G.Y.S.L. project had a clearly identified audience – geography teachers – who had their own professional association and their own networks of contact and information sustained through conferences, journals and training courses, Project Technology had no such potential power-base from which to operate. As David Tawney, the project's official evaluator, observed, it was a project with no fixed abode.

The project could have confined itself to craft teachers, and some voices in the Schools Council clearly expected it to do that, but it found it difficult to identify with craft teachers and seemed wary of the low status such an association would have for them. After all, if its aim was to change one of the central values in curriculum by raising the status of applied studies, becoming boxed off as a craft project would present a trap. Science

108

teachers seemed a more acceptable audience, but at the time most science teachers who might have been interested were heavily involved with Nuffield Science which, as we have seen, was strongly underwritten by the A.S.E., the science teachers' professional association.

Lacking an existing professional network, Project Technology saw the problem of creating one as its main task. It received some impetus when, in 1967, the Duke of Edinburgh, acting independently, set up an 'action group' to stimulate engineering in the schools. The action group was first conceived as an appeal to industry to finance more adequate equipment for applied science teaching in schools. But once the establishment of Project Technology was recognised, the Action Group was reconstituted as the Schools Science and Technology Committee.

Although the S.S.T.C. was not formally a part of Project Technology, there were strong connections. Geoffrey Harrison was a member of the committee and had some hand in writing the committee's terms of reference (which were to seek out the needs of schools, to stimulate activities to meet these needs, to improve the teaching of science and technology in schools and to increase the involvement of pupils in creative technological activity). John Banks of the Schools Council was the committee's secretary, and Edward Semper was also a member. Although the S.S.T.C. had no funds to distribute, it was a high-powered committee whose membership included not only Prince Philip, but Nobel prize winners and captains of industry like Basil de Ferranti. Nor was it just a show piece committee. It met regularly (once a month) over a period of three years.

From Project Technology's point of view perhaps the greatest success of the S.S.T.C. was in setting up the National Centre for School Technology at Trent Polytechnic (with Harrison as director), local science and technology centres (such as those at Sheffield Polytechnic and Southampton University) and the continuing body which succeeded the committee – the Standing Conference on School Science and Technology (S.C.S.S.T.).

The total picture of organisational influence and network is complex: we have only been able to hint at it here. A diagram from one of Project Technology's own publications makes the picture a little clearer:

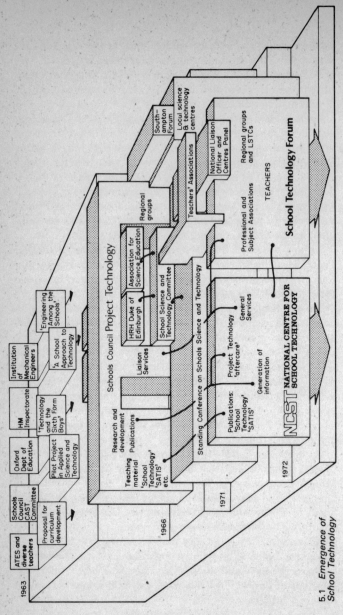

The figure contains the following labels:

1963 — ATES and diverse teachers — Proposal for curriculum development — Schools Council CAST Committee

Oxford Dept of Education — Pilot Project in Applied Science and Technology

HM Inspectorate — "Technology and the Sixth Form Boys"

Institution of Mechanical Engineers — 'A School Approach to Technology' — 'Engineering Among the Schools'

Schools Council Project Technology

Research and development Publications — Teaching material 'School Technology', 'SATIS' etc.

Association for Science Education — HRH Duke of Edinburgh — School Science and Technology Committee — Regional groups — Teachers' Associations — Southampton Forum — Local science & technology centres

Liaison Services

1966

Standing Conference on Schools Science and Technology — 1971

Publications: 'School Technology', 'SATIS' — Generation of information — Project Technology 'aftercare' — General Services

NCST NATIONAL CENTRE FOR SCHOOL TECHNOLOGY — 1972

Professional and Subject Associations — National Liaison Officer and Centres Panel — Regional groups and LSTCs — TEACHERS

School Technology Forum

5.1 Emergence of School Technology

Problems of evaluation

Project Technology's strategy for reform is strikingly different to that of G.Y.S.L. The materials it produced, in part to placate pressures from sponsors and others, do not add up to anything like a total representation of project philosophy.

Any informal attempt to evaluate their strategy keeps running up against the fact that our ideas of success and failure in the curriculum field are (more than we realise) ideas about teaching materials. Basic data on sales, readership, distribution, use, cost and effectiveness simply are not available from a project that seemed mainly concerned to create a social movement.

Formal attempts at evaluation fared little better. The evaluation unit at Keele which attempted to evaluate the project never got beyond defining readership, analysing test results or producing feedback on materials. Evaluating *influence,* which was Project Technology's main aim, is extraordinarily difficult to do, not just technically but because the social processes involved are, by their nature, elusive and time scales are often protracted. The evaluation problem is not just a problem of measurement. In schools and L.E.A.s Project Technology has been highly criticised, not to say condemned. It has been called, with some accuracy, an 'invisible project'. 'It cost £270,000 – the most ever spent on a single project – and had nothing to show for it.' The general impression it gives is of a project that never penetrated the classroom, and so has not touched practice.

Part of our problem is that when we look at planned social change, whether in education or elsewhere, we tend to judge success and failure too soon. Project Technology set out to change a central value in the curriculum (the low status given to applied science) and attempted to do so, not by direct intervention, but by supporting those in the system (particularly teachers) who felt the change was necessary.

As a result, the effects of the project have often been subtle, difficult to identify, and frequently modified by other influences. By their nature, the products of the project lack the kind of purity that can be recognised in published materials. This is inevitable where 'influence' is seen as the key mechanism of change. The National Centre for School Technology is seen as an achievement of Trent Polytechnic as much as it is seen as a product of the project. The regional centre in Sheffield is seen as part of Sheffield Polytechnic. The Open University courses on technology are seen as products of the Open University. The J.M.B. 'A' level course in engineering science is seen as an achievement of the J.M.B. To some extent it is true that they are, but it is also true that without the catalytic effect of Project Technology most of these things would not have happened at all, or, if they had happened, they would have turned out very differently.

The ideas, thoughts and words we bring to bear in judging the success and failure of curriculum projects have considerable analytic purity. We can judge the effectiveness of a pack of materials produced by a project because it seems indivisibly a part of the project. We find it much harder to operate in the kind of world that Project Technology created because its categories seem so imprecise as to lack identifiable referents and ownership of ideas and products is often difficult to identify. But if we step back and ask ourselves which view of the world is closer to the real world as we know and experience it, I think we must admit that the complexity, ambiguity and lack of purity that seem characteristic of Project Technology's world view are closer to the truth than the pure world of product, audience intention and effect which characterise the public statements of most curriculum projects and their sponsors.

The strength of the social interaction model seems to be in its close fit with the real world. Its weakness is perhaps its elusive accountability. On the one hand we can admire the sophisticated social perception of Project Technology and point to the subtlety and complexity of its effects. On the other, we can argue that it would be difficult to spend five years and a quarter of a million pounds and not achieve some effects.

In chapter 6 we point out that the project may have been the victim of fast-changing, large scale events. At a more local level, the immediate audience for the project changed. In the life of the project the Schools Council underwent a transformation from charismatic to bureaucratic leadership. Morrell, Morris and Banks were gone and effective power was in the hands of the N.U.T. Breadth of vision became a quality less valued than useful output in terms of something schools could use without too much difficulty.

Concluding comments

Following Becher's advice we have looked at Project Technology as though it exemplified Havelock's social interaction model, and certainly much of what Becher predicts can be found in the effects and experience of the project. When the project succeeded in creating networks it often found itself unable to control them. One result was that many of its publications simply disappeared into the system. And when it did succeed in sparking off developments outside its own aegis, the project felt unable to claim them as successes without destroying the logic of the model. Geoffrey Harrison commented in an interview:

> The whole point of the Regional Centres is that they must come as local initiatives. Therefore the setting up of those centres is something you have to forget as having to do with a national initiative from Project Technology. It has taken a great deal of our time to talk to local committees about what is required in the form of local support, but that's not part of the public success of Project Technology.
>
> (SAFARI interview 1974)

The philosophy of support eloquently articulated by Harrison was widely interpreted by others as a lack of direction and control from the centre. Many of those involved in the project, both in schools and in the Schools Council, were unable to escape the assumptions of the R, D and D model. They listened to the rhetoric of the social interaction model but still expected the materials to arrive. In the end, when no materials appeared, they became confused, disappointed and cynical. '£270,000 and nothing to show for it' became a common judgement on the project.

We asked one headmaster, a man who did not seem a natural cynic, what his experience of the project had been. He explained that his school (a secondary modern) had been involved in a cooperative venture with two neighbouring schools, a boys' grammar school and a public school. Working under the direction of the conservation officer of the local canal (a retired naval officer), the boys had designed and built a craft for clearing water weed. The public school had made the weed cutting gear, the grammar school had designed the boat, and his school had built it. When the time came to launch the boat his boys could not be there. We asked him what had happened. 'The boat?', he said. 'It sank. Just like Project Technology.'

While disappointment was a common reaction at the periphery (though certainly not universal), the response from the centre was much stronger. Project Technology touched some tender political sensitivities at the Schools Council. When Geoffrey Harrison dispersed his autonomy through the support network, he in effect crossed territorial boundaries. At one point early in the project, the team wanted to set up a particular regional group in a rural county. Harrison was aware that this could be a risky operation and was anxious to identify someone who would be 'sympathetic, had the right attitudes and the right enthusiasm'. Receiving little response from the L.E.A.s and the technical colleges, he discovered that someone known to the team from the pilot study had recently been appointed principal of a suitably located city college. The approach to this man, asking if he would take the initiative in the area, was followed by a letter from the Schools Council demanding to know why the project hadn't approached a particular county technical college, which the writer knew well and deemed more appropriate. Harrison quoted the letter as ending with these words: 'It is time that those at the periphery of the Schools Council understood what was required of them from the centre'.

The Schools Council may grant projects autonomy even when they don't perceive it (Shipman suggests that the Keele Project interpreted the Council's granting of autonomy as lack of interest and enthusiasm). Projects cannot be fully autonomous, however, since they inevitably act as agencies of the Schools Council, so that when their actions question the basis of Council structure, direction and policy, the Council itself has to act correctively: hence the apparent over-reaction to Harrison's regional initiative.

We cannot close this chapter without raising some doubts about the equation of Project Technology and the social interaction model. It can be argued that Harrison was aware of the objections Becher was later to raise against the model, and that the model he implemented was rather different from a pure social interaction model such as Havelock and Becher envisage.

When we look at the people who constitute the network, it is evident that the most prominent names are often institutions, organisations and committees, rather than the names of individuals. The enduring achievements of the project have been less in the generation of networks of individuals and more in the creation of organisations and institutions. Schon sees the strength of the interaction model in its ease of replacement in a fast changing world. By contrast, Project Technology created a set of permanent institutions, which are by virtue of their permanence only rarely capable of the flexibility and adaptability

114

needed in the face of social and cultural change.

Two comments must be added before leaving Project Technology. The first is that Project Technology's intellectual grasp of the curriculum problem may well be more sophisticated than that of other projects, even if it is not easily accessible in its published statements. The question remains, however, of whether a more sophisticated analysis could have led to better informed action, or to more effective change. In the field of curriculum reform (as in other areas of social change) a blunt instrument wielded with enough force is likely to change something, even if it is in ways that cannot be predicted or controlled. Ultimately, judgements about effectiveness can only be made in the long term. In general terms, Project Technology seems to have been judged by most people as a failure in the short run, and Nuffield Science and G.Y.S.L. as successes. But we have to remember that a decade is a short time in social change.

The second comment is that the pure analytic category model of curriculum change is the one we usually call 'the engineering model'. It is, after all, a view of the world which sees social events and processes as machine-like systems which can be controlled through the application of rational designs. We leave it simply as a paradox that the one British project which effectively broke out of the engineering model in terms of its thinking about planning educational change was a project in the field of engineering, partly staffed by engineers.

Further reading
The most concise single source on Project Technology is a book of readings published for the Open University 'Technology for Teachers' Course (Marshall 1974). It consists of a range of extracts from the journal *School Technology*.

6 RHETORIC AND REALITY IN CURRICULUM RENEWAL

Events and trends: a backcloth

In monitoring the process of curriculum change through curriculum projects it is necessary to take into account a backcloth of recent events and current trends if we are to understand what is happening. What would an outline catalogue of the events most likely to impinge on the world of curriculum projects look like? The SAFARI project attempted such a list in 1974:

(1) The raising of the school leaving age to sixteen. Written into the 1944 Act but only implemented in 1972.

(2) Local government reorganisation. As of 1 April 1974 (one year later in Scotland) fewer, larger authorities were established and considerable continuing internal reorganisation took effect.

(3) The trend towards comprehensive secondary schooling, which was begun in the early sixties, continued so that currently about half the secondary school population attend comprehensive schools.

(4) The trend towards comprehensive schooling tended to *increase* the range of variation within the system rather than to standardise it. Some authorities introduced middle schools, and did so for children of different ages. Some introduced sixth form colleges, some 11-18 comprehensives. With local government reorganisation the picture was further complicated because a new authority could contain two or three different systems as legacies from the previous authorities.

(5) The trend towards larger secondary schools has often led to internal structural changes in the schools. Role infla-

tion and specialisation of function has often removed an increasing number of staff from the classroom for a larger proportion of their time. In some ways this has had the effect of moving British schools closer to the American pattern.

(6) The general mood of reform in the mid and late sixties led a small number of (mostly newly established) secondary schools to develop distinct innovating climates. Often they attracted unusually well-qualified staff and through wide publicity they were seen to set trends for the rest of the system (e.g. Countesthorpe, Stantonbury, Abraham Moss . . .).

(7) There has been a general expansion of L.E.A. advisory services, especially expanding the role of advisers in relation to the support of curriculum development projects. Science and humanities have been noticeably prominent in this respect. The appointment of advisory teachers and the establishment of teachers' centres has reinforced the trend.

(8) Examinations and assessment procedures have always acted an an important constraint on the 'myth of autonomy'. From the first days of Nuffield Science, examination reform has been a key target for curriculum reform. Changes have been both evident and imminent. C.S.E. exams have proliferated and most G.C.E. boards have been involved in setting new exams and developing new styles of examining. It is difficult to judge the effect of numerous Schools Council efforts in this field; the arguments that they have had both conservative and progressive effects appear fairly equally balanced.

(9) Radical changes in the organisation of teacher education have been suggested and discussed. (The James Report and the resulting Government White Paper *Education: A Framework for Expansion*)

(10) A sense of crisis (widely reported by the Press, supported by some teacher unions and fed by *Black Paper* critics) has arisen in urban schools, particularly in Inner London.

(11) Recent economic cutbacks have especially affected the funds available for curriculum development and support, which was mainly marginal money. This seems especially important at local authority level and affects indirect as

well as direct support (for example through the reduction of secondments for attendance of courses).

(12) There has been a general move in secondary schools towards team teaching, integrated studies, mixed ability grouping, informal teaching methods, and the establishment of resource-based learning. This trend has often been inextricably linked with curriculum development, but not necessarily tied to particular projects.

(13) Within sponsoring bodies there has been a trend towards funding small-scale local and regional projects rather than expensive national projects.

(14) As the early projects have become established and their key staff moved to more central roles in the system, so routines have become more bureaucratic and the field of curriculum development more politicised.

(15) There has been a growing concern with educational issues arising from the intake into secondary schools of a large number of children of immigrant origin.

Marginal enterprises

Curriculum development projects are short-term enterprises, usually funded for three years. They are institutionally precarious, attached to a university or college of education but rarely part of it. They offer only a transitory existence, marking transitional points in the careers of team members rather than permanent posts. Even a project's contact with the stable real world outside itself is equivocal. Most people meet the project as a glossy pack of materials or as a well-rehearsed performance by a team member at a project conference. In contrast, those who visit the project at its home base find it housed in a way that reflects its marginal status. Projects have been in huts hidden behind the garden sheds (Keele), in students' residences (G.Y.S.L. at Avery Hill), isolated in a variety of annexes. Amongst those least likely to win architectural awards are the old factory three miles from the main college which houses Science at Chelsea, and the virtually-deserted temporary building (remaining from the University's founding years) which houses the Humanities Project in East Anglia.

In every sense projects are temporary structures. Their status is marginal. They need to create national networks across isolated and autonomous institutions in a short time. They are vulnerable as organisations and also create vulnerability for the individuals within them. It is not surprising therefore that projects offer different messages to different segments of their audience. These messages are negotiated into a system of shared meanings which will also appear differently to the different audiences. A project will be perceived in a way that reflects both its own 'impression management' and the assumptions of the receivers through which the impressions are screened. We have described this process in our account of the dissemination of the Geography for the Young School Leaver Project.

In this chapter we add another dimension to the picture we have given of curriculum negotiation. In a climate of rapid change, marginal organisations are particularly vulnerable to shifts of policy, both educational and economic. They are in the firing line, and must respond flexibly in order to survive. It is easy to predict therefore that the newly-funded project will be sensitive to its historical and contemporary context, will weigh up trends and possible futures. But it also has to act now, because it will be judged tomorrow. The project director, like the editor of a newspaper, has to weigh up interest in the flood of passing events, to make some sense of it and press it into some sort of accessible meaning before the situation changes. The project, like the newspaper, reports, creates and distributes the news. The accent is on a pragmatism, with some willingness to cut corners. For example, 'design' in curriculum research and development may be less rational and scientific than one would suppose, and more a matter of backing hunches. Projects, then, are both visions and versions of the present. They are situation-dependent.

A major consequence of this is that projects are continuously at the mercy of unforeseen events. They are also at the mercy of their friends. Once the first curriculum projects were established within the education system it became clear that they were being met with ambivalence by those whose task it was to manage the innovations once the project team disbanded. Heads of schools, local authority officers and individual teachers soon learnt that curriculum innovation stimulated demand as often as it satisfied it. The same people who initially encouraged project development often found themselves having to act to contain it, in order to retain some control over their own roles within the system. This is the paradox of curriculum reform. Stimulus can go hand in hand with containment. Support is an equivocal concept. It will be withheld by those most committed to offering it once they find themselves unable to control the complexities of their own environment. One of the effects of the Nuffield Science Teaching Project was to stimulate the appointment of science advisers, inspectors, advisory teachers and teachers' centre wardens in the L.E.A.s. To those involved in curriculum development this seemed a clear case of success. Kevin Keohane, overall coordinator of the project, pointed to the successful outcomes of the projects and singled out 'teachers' centres and the growth of science advisory services, which contribute to the development of curricula in schools and help to accentuate change'. From the project point of view the appointment of the science advisers looked to be a move for expansion, particularly as the people appointed were often former project team members or trial school teachers who were able to run in-service training courses that were virtually dissemination courses for the projects they had just left. Considerable role conflict must have been faced by the science advisers who had been project team members and who now found themselves reminded by the authority that they were local government officers who, though their sympathies might be with the schools, owed their loyalty to the Education Committee. And the conflict must have been heightened in the last few years as inflation and economic stringency have cut into the funds available for curriculum development and as advisory services as a whole have found themselves pushed more and more into evaluation roles.

On being overtaken by events

Curriculum development is not continuous but jerky and haphazard. Moreover at the project level it frequently involves 'freezing' a planned innovation in order to 'develop' (i.e. test) it. This freezing of an approach to a curriculum problem or the stabilising of assumptions about its educational context leaves the project in permanent danger of being overtaken by events. The 'O' level projects in physics, chemistry and biology which formed the first phase of the Nuffield Science Teaching Project were initiated in the late fifties and early sixties by active members of the Science Masters' Association (S.M.A.). At this time 'O' level science teaching was confined to grammar and public schools. Some secondary modern schools were beginning to

120

introduce science but few taught it to 'O' level. One of the main issues surrounding the projects was the extent of specialisation in science (especially in sixth forms). The projects were initiated around the time of the intellectual controversy between Snow and Leavis over the claims of science as an element of Culture (with a capital 'C'). During their development the 'claims of science' controversy became increasingly economic. It focussed on the 'swing from science' in schools and colleges. There was also increased concern about a national shortage of scientific manpower. The country needed more specialist scientists and scientifically-imaginative administrators, managers, and politicians than it was producing. The climate suggested a revitalisation of science education at all levels, but the 'O' level projects found themselves trapped in a single prestigious stratum. The projects were consciously intended for (and quickly identified with) an elite selection of the school population – what Ernest Coulson of the chemistry 'O' level team (and later organiser of the 'A' level project) was to call 'grammar school streams' in whatever kind of school they happened to be located.

In retrospect we can define these projects as conservative (Ernest Coulson prefers to describe himself as a 'conservationist'), though at the time it must have seemed more like pragmatism. In Coulson's own judgement: 'The projects are most successful when they do not get too far ahead of present thought and practice. The teaching profession as a whole, especially the non-vocal majority, are rightly more susceptible to evolution than to revolution' (Coulson 1972). Philosophically and logically the position adopted appeared to be a sound one but historically it may have been the wrong point at which to stand. The irony of history is quite explicit. The projects found themselves being published just as a Labour Government came to power and set in motion the reorganisation of secondary schooling. Schools were being changed in ways that left the 'O' level projects behind rather than ahead of events. But it would be wrong to blame the projects for the shortfall. That comprehensive secondary schooling would be rapidly implemented, that many of the new comprehensives would move to integrated and unified science courses, developing C.S.E. rather than G.C.E. exams, simply formed no part of the predictable future in the educational climate that gave birth to the projects in the late fifties and early sixties.

On being swamped by fashion

Curriculum projects usually aspire to far more than reform of the curriculum; they nurse ideologies of reform in the organisation of the school and in the nature of education itself. But the early Nuffield Science Projects were more narrowly *curriculum* reform projects prepared to take the education system as they found it rather than to pursue its transformation. Other projects made substantially higher demands organisationally. They needed the impetus of prevailing fashion. But what is carried along on one wave may be swamped by the next.

Project Technology provides an interesting example of a project riding the surf on one wave of fashion, but appearing to be engulfed by a succeeding wave of a different character. Looking forward to the possibility of E.E.C. entry Harold Wilson had led a strong campaign to emphasise the scientific and technological contribution Britain would make to a future Europe, supporting a high standard of living based on science-based industry. (Britain was the only European country with its own computer industry.) Once in power the government instituted the new 'Ministry of Technology' and began its bid for scientific and technological leadership in Europe with joint projects like Concorde.

The connection between an embryo curriculum project and political events at a national level may seem far-fetched but both were products of, and contributors to, a particular national mood. As we have seen, at one point the connection actually became concrete. Edward Semper, campaigning for curriculum development in the field of applied science and finding it difficult to get responses from officials in the D.E.S., was inspired by the politicians' enthusiasm to write to the new prime minister outlining his case. He received a quick reply, followed by a 'phone call from the D.E.S. apologising for 'losing his letter' and the setting up of a meeting with the joint secretaries of the newly-formed Schools Council.

Changes in fashion and mood are by nature elusive if we are considering notions as abstract as technological ideology, but a summarised account of the shift can certainly be attempted. The project rode in on one wave of fashion but in its own lifetime new events caused the climate to change. The political campaigns moved on to fresh issues (rising prices, inflation, devaluation of the pound . . .). By the early and mid-seventies the image of technology too had changed. No longer seen as the tool and index of advanced civilisation, it even took on some of the imagery of a disease. The conservation and ecology movements came to prominence, reaching even B.B.C.'s 'Tomorrow's World'. The word 'technology' took on new images and new connotations. Neil Armstrong had taken his step on the surface of the moon. Sputnik was finally seen as a primitive earth satellite. Space research was reduced merely to a scientific enterprise. The stronger, insistent image of technology was the one that came from the Vietnam war: inhuman, corrupting and destructive on an unprecedented scale. The crisis of technological man came with the fuel crisis, the rapid increase in fuel costs seeming to threaten basic values in our culture. After a generation of cars with names like Jaguar, Cougar and Tiger, VW brought out a model they marketed as 'The Rabbit'!

We are not arguing that the definitions and meanings of the term 'technology' used by the project changed, or that conservation arguments destroyed their case. Far from it; what changed were the public images associated with the project. For example, in the early days of the project the Duke of Edinburgh supported the teaching of technology in schools. He may yet, but what now reaches the media is that he supports wildlife conservation. The messages of the two movements may not be logically dissonant, but in their wider associations they carry quite different meanings. It could be argued that such associations do not impinge on something as self-contained as a curriculum development project. We believe that they are important and that they do touch what people do in classrooms, becoming real in the motivations, interests and enthusiasms of teachers and pupils. Geoffrey Harrison made the same point when he claimed that a major task of Project Technology was to 'change attitudes to technology'.

Changes in the L.E.A.s
Given the situation that has developed in the two or three years up to 1975, we cannot leave the theme of cultural change without looking more directly at the current situation at local authority level. Local government has undergone two major structural changes in recent years. Following the Redcliffe Maud Report the number of authorities was reduced and new units formed by local government reorganisation (as it came to be called), often coalescing urban and rural areas.

Reorganisation created its own problems and, as we have seen, some of the new authorities found themselves with highly complex education systems created by the collision of previously very different forms of organisation. There were also a number of temporary problems that arose simply from the fact of reorganisation. One G.Y.S.L. training conference began the day that reorganisation came into effect. Somewhat to the embarrassment of the organisers, they found that one of the new authorities had sent two coordinators and two teams of teachers (one from each of the old L.E.A.s) and that they were oblivious of each other's existence until the conference itself.

The Bains Report saw in the 1974 boundary changes an opportunity to create quite radical changes in the structure of local government. Although retaining a distinction between elected members and appointed officers, Bains suggested changes in the structure of local government, arguing for inter-departmental coordination on the lines of what in industry was known as a 'corporate management' model. Corporate management involves the formation of cross-departmental committees, horizontal movement of staff at management level, and a general move towards policy evaluation.

Commitment to long-term plans is not a strong tradition in local government where the next election can bring major reversals of policy (see Saran 1974). Nor is it encouraged by budgeting systems that operate on a year-to-year basis. Tyrell Burgess, writing about the effects of reorganisation one month after it came into effect (*Guardian*, 7 May 1974), noted that 'it was not until February that the local authorities knew the basis on which they could budget for the year beginning one month later', and added that, in times of rapid inflation, 'it is not a cliché to say that if English Government can survive this, they can survive anything.'

The systematisation and integration of local government functions seems a rational step to take. The consequences for curriculum development are, however, worth studying. Education absorbs a large proportion of local government expenditure (between sixty and eighty per cent), most of which is accounted for in fixed costs. An important effect of Bains-type reorganisation has been to move many financial decisions out of the departments into integrated sub-committees which deal not just with education budgets, but with all major items of local government spending. Given the fact that education has always had the largest share of the budget, it is inevitable that educational spending will come under particularly heavy scrutiny.

One important effect of the concentration of power in small integrated committees, which control (particularly) finance and staffing, has been the promotion of a distinctive set of management values. Kershaw, writing in *Public Finance and Accounting* (November 1974), points out that the 'corporate management' structure advocated by Bains

> entails at the very least a high degree of centralisation of policy making, analysis and review . . . [in which] . . . the new management elite . . . must take an overview of the authority's activities as a whole and create a framework of policy and strategy within which individual departments and committees must work and by which they must be assessed.

Education comes under pressure because traditionally it enjoys a major share of the budget, but it also finds it difficult to make a strong case for many of its activities because their outcomes are not always easily assessed within the kinds of 'framework' Kershaw identifies. The work of the advisory services provides a typical example. They have no real equivalents in other local government departments, and their formal job descriptions do not really describe adequately what they do. The essence of their job is to promote 'quality' within the sysem, involving tasks not easily assessed in terms of gains per unit cost.

In this situation it is quite possible that education may find itself slipping on a trend that Ralph James has observed in industry, where large companies operating under corporate management tend to decentralise to 'profit centres'. Such centres have functions which fit most comfortably within the 'framework'. They are able to utilise the language, values and concerns of key sub-committees, and in consequence develop considerable autonomy within general policy constraints. James suggests that in local government there may be a corresponding decentralisation to 'cost-effective' centres, perhaps with accountants 'participating as team members . . . rather than as instruments of the control system' (*Education*, 30 March 1973).

Another possible effect of corporate management which has consequences for curriculum innovation is its effect on the relationships between officers and members. Tyrell Burgess, for

125

instance, has argued (in the *Guardian*, 7 May 1974) that one effect of corporate management is to complicate the affairs of committees and create problems of understanding for the part-time elected member, making 'it harder than ever for the representatives to control the officials'.

At one time it must have seemed as though the L.E.A.s were taking the initiative from the projects and providing continuity for curriculum development. Support was not restricted to enabling schools to implement the science projects, but extended beyond the recommended books and equipment to money for lab technicians, extra teachers and new buildings. In one authority at least, the £40,000 a year the science adviser could distribute as 'Nuffield Science Money' was only loosely tied to the implementation of particular projects.

Seen from the L.E.A. point of view the picture is rather more complex. The Nuffield Science Projects often required consider-able investment in equipment, buildings, materials and staff. Instead of a few sets of demonstration equipment teachers needed class sets, so that the *children* could do the experiments instead of the teachers. Instead of using microscopes only with the sixth forms they needed class sets from the first year upwards. Storage and preparation became logistic problems; schools needed new prep rooms and qualified technical assis-tants. Few Authorities were able to meet all the demands that the stimulus of the projects generated, yet the Authorities them-selves were often unable to create policies which evaluated priorities as demands began to proliferate. One school might be granted funds for laser equipment, or for a planetarium, but as a senior H.M.I. wryly commented, you had to have someone who could say 'No' to the others. Some specialist advisers found to their dismay that they were expected to dampen down rather than stimulate development.

Just as the growth and development of the curriculum reform movement now looks to have been dependent on economic expansion, so economic recession has created a new mood and a new situation. At the national level (at the time of writing) pressure within the cabinet on the Secretary of State for Educa-tion must be considerable, especially given a Labour Govern-ment faced with increasing unemployment and working hard to retain consensus with the T.U.C. Local government finds itself caught in a squeeze between mounting public concern over

126

increasing rates and strong government pressure to reduce spending.

Given the coincidence of political and lay scrutiny of educational spending there has been considerable interest in different forms of accountability. When the D.E.S. in 1974 set up a small unit to work in the field of assessment of academic performance (A.P.U.), this was widely interpreted as an indication of future trends and the beginnings of a bid for central control of education.

Other voices, too, talk of increasing centralisation. Some senior L.E.A. administrators predict that corporate management within the L.E.A.s will force education out of local government and into a closer relationship with the D.E.S. One commentator sees the possibility that large-scale salary increases to teachers (under the Houghton Award) will reinforce calls for accountability. It is not only the administration that may be held accountable but also the individual school and the individual teacher.

These comments are highly speculative and we report them only in the hope that we can to some extent avoid being overtaken by events, though inevitably that will be our fate. One of the problems of reflexive predictions is that they become part of the context from which prediction is made.

What we can say with some certainty is that the curriculum reform movement which began in this country with the Nuffield Science Teaching Project, and which went on through the creation of the Schools Council to affect almost every corner of the school curriculum, has now run its course in its present form. It is unlikely that in the near future we will again see the funding of large-scale central projects like the Humanities Curriculum Project and Project Technology.

Judging the effects of the movement is difficult. As we have shown, the situation is more complex than it seemed at first sight. Almost all new inventions arise out of the stream of history, and are 'new' only to contemporary observers; this being so, they carry more messages than their inventors attempt to communicate in their first formulations, or even understand.

The curriculum in the schools has been affected by the efforts and experience of the projects, which have also reflected and contributed to changes in the educational system at large. But the task of evaluating the direction and the extent of these

127

changes will remain for historians of our time. We have attempted to provide some data.

Economic stringency

The trends outlined in the previous section provide a background against which the effects of inflation and economic stringency on curriculum innovation can be examined. There is no doubt that as we write the effects of economic stringency are only just beginning to be felt, and that any examples we give are likely to be overtaken by events by the time this book reaches the reader. Yet already we can see that the kind of savings that education committees are able to make tend to be painful gestures. In the winter of 1974, for example, Sheffield extended its school Christmas holidays by one week in order to save fuel costs, and suspended evening classes for a month for similar reasons. In February 1974 Ewan Carr, chairman of the Inner London Education Authority's Finance Subcommittee, introduced the most highly scrutinised I.L.E.A. budget of the decade, providing estimates for an annual expenditure of £370m. Although the authority had earlier called for 'a thorough review of expenditure' and the I.L.E.A. had cut its budget to 'no growth in real terms over the previous year', the actual cuts meant that 'numerous projects and improvements which are very necessary and we considered desirable have been deferred'. When itemised all these cuts seem to be in areas where the return was arguably greater than the saving, for they included in-service training for teachers, the I.L.E.A.s educational television service, and the grant to the University of London. Inevitably, cuts in marginal areas are likely to be most critical for curriculum development, which is itself seen as a marginal activity.

As recently as 1969 when the Humanities Project held a conference for L.E.A. representatives to initiate its dissemination programme, its claims on resources (which included all teaching in half-classes) were generally seen as feasible and reasonable. No project could expect a similar welcome in 1976. As Jack Wrigley wrote in his open letter to the new chairman of the Schools Council, 'some of the essentials of ten years ago now look like luxuries' (*Times Educational Supplement,* 26 September 1975).

If the scene is bleak at the implementation end of the innovation system, it seems worse at the source. The Nuffield Foundation

128

was able to initiate curriculum reform in the early sixties because of the prosperity of the motor industry and because government agencies were increasingly taking over its traditional funding policies (in medical research, for example). In 1975, with British Leyland shares paying almost no dividends, Nuffield have virtually ceased funding in education and Tony Becher, the assistant director of the Foundation who steered through the reforms of the early sixties, has left for a chair at Sussex and has not been replaced.

The Schools Council has slowed down and faces an uncertain future. Universities, colleges of education and polytechnics have virtually ceased appointing staff. Curriculum development as a route for academic promotion has effectively closed.

Beyond austerity

This chapter has explored the vicissitudes of a number of curriculum projects against a background of significant educational events. The exploration has served to sharpen the gap between educational rhetoric and educational practice. Beyond the temporary structure of the curriculum project a number of aspirations, themselves situational, have had a hard job struggling to survive in a world changed by shifts in outside political, economic and social forces and by shifts in educational fashion or culturally-related imagery of a more general kind.

The remaining question, beyond the economic crisis, is whether the pattern of curriculum development, as institutionalised over the last decade, is a model that we would want to stay with for the next thrust forward in curriculum renewal. Other models compete for our attention, from the over-reaching macro-project (half collective, half funding agency) like the National Development Programme in Computer Assisted Learning, to the small-scale situation-based explorations that fall under the umbrella heading 'school-based curriculum development'. But certainly when this choice faces us we will not be left without knowledge of what happens inside the educational service to project-inspired ideas once the project itself has folded its tents. Also we shall by then be able to approach, tentatively, the question of understanding the curriculum reform movement as a social system with its own rhetorics and realities, as well as an instrument for giving shape to the more focused purposes and intents of others.

References and
Name index

ATKIN, M. J. (1970) *Curriculum Design: The Central Development Group and the Local Teacher*. Kiel, W. Germany, Institut fur die Pädagogik der Naturwissenschaften Invitational Symposium. *25, 27*

BANKS, J. (1968) House memorandum to Schools Council staff (unpublished). *48*

BECHER, A. (1971) The Dissemination and Implementation of Educational Innovation. Annual Meeting of the British Association for the Advancement of Science, Section L, September 1971 (unpublished). *11, 24, 74, 99, 103, 112, 114*

BEDDIS, R. (1972) *Times Educational Supplement*, 28 April 1972. *55*

BEDDIS, R. (1973) *Times Educational Supplement*, 11 May 1973. *55*

BERGER, J. (1972) *Ways of Seeing*. Harmondsworth, Penguin. *38, 81*

BROCK, W. H. (1971) Prologue to Heurism. In the History of Education Society, *The Changing Curriculum*. London, Methuen. *93, 95, 100*

BROUDY, H. S. (1972) *The Real World of the Public Schools*. New York, Harcourt Brace, Jovanovich Inc. *24, 25, 41, 75, 83*

CARLSON, R. O. (1965) *Adoption of Educational Innovations*. Eugene, Oregon, Centre for the Advanced Study of Educational Administration, University of Oregon. *6*

CLARK, R. W. (1972) *A Biography of the Nuffield Foundation*. London, Longman. *88*

COULSON, E. (1972) *Confessions of a Forward-Looking Educational Conservationist*. Inaugural lecture. Chelsea College, University of London. *95–6, 121*

CREMIN, L. A. (1961) *The Transformation of the School*. New York, Vintage Books. *41*

FANTINI, M. (1970) The Emergence of the Community as an Agent of Urban School Reform. In Foshay, A. W. (ed.) *The Professional as Educator*. New York, Teachers College Press. *28*

FORD TEACHING PROJECT (1973-5) Mimeo. Norwich, Centre for Applied Research in Education, University of East Anglia. *12*

FRYMIER, J. R. (1969) *Fostering Educational Change*. Columbus, Ohio, Merrill. *27*

GEOGRAPHY FOR THE YOUNG SCHOOL LEAVER PROJECT (1974) *Teachers Talking.* Mimeo. G.Y.S.L., Avery Hill College of Education, London S.E.9. *84*

GOODLAD, J. I. (1966) *The Changing School Curriculum.* New York, The Georgian Press for the Fund for the Advancement of Education. *25*

GOODLAD, J. I. (1967) The Reform Movement. In *Rational Planning in Curriculum and Instruction.* New York, National Education Association. *25, 27*

GROBMAN, H. (1970) *Developmental Curriculum Projects.* New York, F. E. Peacock. *41, 99*

HAGERSTRAND, T. (1953) *The Propagation of Innovation Waves.* Lund, Royal University of Sweden. *19*

HAVELOCK, R. G. (1971) *Planning for Innovation through the Dissemination and Utilisation of Knowledge.* Ann Arbor, Centre for Research and Utilisation of Knowledge. *5, 8, 11, 18, 21, 31, 38, 44, 96, 103, 112, 114*

HIGGINBOTTOM, T. (1975) Managing the change. Paper given to C.R.I.T.E. Conference, September 1975. *51, 52, 56*

HOUSE, E. (1974) *The Politics of Educational Innovation.* Berkeley, Calif., McCutchan Publishing Corporation. *5, 12, 18–22, 25, 26, 30, 40, 100*

HUMBLE, S. and SIMONS, H. (in preparation) *From Council to Classroom.* London, Schools Council. *36*

INKELES, A. (1964) *What is Sociology?* New York, Prentice Hall (Foundations of Modern Sociology Series). *6*

JENCKS, C. (1963) Schoolmaster Rickover. *New Republic,* **148**, No 9. *31*

JENKINS, D. R. AND SHIPMAN, M. D. (1976) *Curriculum: an introduction.* London, Open Books. *32*

KERR, J. F. (1967) *The Changing School Curriculum.* London. University of London Press. *34*

KOGAN, M. (1974) *The Politics of Education.* Harmondsworth, Penguin. *33*

LAWSON, J. and SILVER, H. (1973) *A Social History of Education in England.* London, Methuen. *90, 100*

LAYTON, D. (1973) *Science for the People.* London, Allen and Unwin. *91, 100*

McLURE, J. S. (1965) *Educational Documents.* London, Methuen. *93*

McLURE, J. S. (1968) *Curriculum Innovation in Practice.* London, H.M.S.O. *32*

MANZER, R. A. (1970) *Teachers and Politics.* Manchester, Manchester University Press. *33, 34*

MARSHALL, A. R. (1974) (ed.) *School Technology in Action.* London, English University Press. *115*

MILES, M. B. (1964) *Innovation in Education.* Columbia, Ohio, Teachers College Press. *5, 6, 22, 24, 26, 31*

MUSGROVE, F. (1975) The Curriculum for a World of Change. In Taylor, P. H. and Walton, J. (eds), *The Curriculum: Research Innovation and Change.* London, Ward Lock. *87*

131

NATIONAL INSTITUTE OF EDUCATION (1973) *Building Capacity for Renewal and Reform.* Washington D.C., National Institute of Education. *30, 31*

NISBET, J. (1970) Curriculum development in Scotland. *Journal of Curriculum Studies,* **2**, No 1. *33, 34, 35, 41*

NUFFIELD CHEMISTRY (1967) *Handbook for Teachers.* Longman/Penguin. *75, 93*

ORGANISATION FOR ECONOMIC AND CULTURAL DEVELOPMENT (1971) *The Management of Innovation in Education.* Paris, O.E.C.D. *36, 42*

PAGE, G. T. (1968) *Engineering Among the Schools.* London, Institution of Mechanical Engineers. *104, 105, 106, 107*

ROGERS, E. M. (1962) *The Diffusion of Innovations.* New York, Free Press. *8, 16, 17, 22*

ROGERS, E. M. and SHOEMAKER, F. F. (1971) *Communication of Innovations: a Cross-Cultural Approach.* 2nd edition. New York, Free Press; London, Macmillan. *5, 6, 7, 13, 18, 21, 22*

RUDDUCK, J. (in preparation) *Dissemination in Practice.* London, Schools Council. *15, 36*

SAFARI (1974) *Innovation, Evaluation and Research and the Problem of Control.* Norwich, Centre for Applied Research in Education, University of East Anglia (mimeo). *ix, 76, 82, 96, 97, 98, 103, 113*

SARAN, R. (1974) *Policy-making in Secondary Education: a Case Study.* Oxford, Clarendon Press. *124*

SCHON, D. A. (1971) *Beyond the Stable State: Public and Private Learning in a Changing Society.* Harmondsworth, Penguin. *5, 12–18, 22, 39, 40, 47, 103, 114*

SCHOOLS COUNCIL (1973, 1974, 1975) G.Y.S.L. Theme One: *Man, Land and Leisure;* Theme Two: *Cities and People;* Theme Three: *People, Place and Work.* London, Thomas Nelson. *84*

SCHOOLS COUNCIL (1973) *Pattern and Variations in Curriculum Development Projects.* London, Macmillan. *41, 84*

SCHOOL TECHNOLOGY FORUM (1973) *Working Paper No 1.* Nottingham, Standing Conference on School Science and Technology. *x, 110*

SCIENCE MASTERS ASSOCIATION AND A.W.S.T. (1961) *Science and Education: A Policy Statement.* London, John Murray. *87, 88*

SHIPMAN, M. (1974) *Inside a Curriculum Project.* London, Methuen. *36, 38, 39, 41, 84, 114*

STENHOUSE, L. (1975) *An Introduction to Curriculum Research and Development.* London, Heinemann. *11, 14, 18, 50*

WALFORD, R. (1973) *New Directions in Geography Teaching.* London, Longmans. *54*

WARING, M. (1975) Aspects of the Dynamics of Curriculum Reform. Ph.D. thesis. University of London. *100*

132

Subject index